P=D: PROSPECTING = DATING.
MAKE THEM CHASE YOU.

TABLE OF CONTENTS

INTRODUCTION:

THIS WAS NEVER PROSPECTING. THIS WAS FOREPLAY

"Desire is not something you can force."

– Esther Perel

Cold calling didn't die.

The lessons that made it work just started getting handed down like bad group-project advice from people who haven't been "picked first" for something since 2007.

Same thing with dating. People stopped teaching how to do that properly long before Tinder started clogging up everybody's phones with messages like "Hey, I lost my number, can I have yours?"

We have more tools, more channels, and more ways to reach out. *Great.* We also somehow have less honesty and less chemistry between people than you'd find in a high school hallway.

It's one giant group chat where everyone saw the message, nobody replied, and somehow everybody's still pretending the vibes are amazing.

Yes, this is a sales-and-dating book. And yes, somewhere a LinkedIn influencer just felt a disturbance in the force because this is exactly the kind of thing they'd label "cringe," right before posting a carousel about authenticity that sounds like it was ghostwritten by a beige wall and formatted by Canva Premium.

That's why this book exists.

And before somebody with a podcast mic and a moral panic gets cute: this is not a book about manipulation. Manipulation is what people grasp for when they have no signal, no timing, and no nerve. This is about reading pressure honestly, saying the true thing cleanly, and not groveling for approval like the world owes you something.

The point is to notice when the room is already leaning, stop poisoning with need, and let the right people respond to something real.

If the mood isn't there, the move should die.

Good. Let it.

Nobody really had the range to do this right. Or the nerve to connect the dots properly. Maybe I'm not the first guy to say dating and sales share something. Still, a good chunk of what's already out there is either awkward, too tactical, or written like HR found out people flirt and immediately tried to build a framework with role-play exercises, laminated values, and a PDF called *Connection at Scale.*

No thanks.

This isn't a sales book wearing romance as a Halloween costume and throwing in a few opinions about "love bombing" to feel current.

It's a book about attention, tension, validation, withdrawal, timing, self-control, and the tiny silent decisions people make before they say a single honest thing out loud.

Think something closer to *Euphoria* than a cute sales playbook.

Why? Because that whole show, under all the glitter, eyeliner, and soundtrack abuse, is really about one thing: who wants who more, who knows it, and who loses control first.

That's dating. It's also outbound sales.

Honestly, it's most human interaction once the stakes are high enough.

Everybody on that show accidentally teaches prospecting better than most sales trainers.

Rue shows you what happens when your emotional state is driving the car: you're done before you leave the driveway. Jules understands that tension pulls harder than pursuit. Cassie is what happens when you overinvest, lose your mind, and call it passion because "I'm humiliating myself in real time" sounds more cinematic. Nate, awful as he is, proves a brutal truth: the person who needs less usually controls more. Fez barely says anything and still owns the room because calm certainty beats blabbering every single time.

That's not TV commentary. That's your pipeline.

Deals don't die because you forgot a rebuttal. They die because the other person felt your need and decided to change the channel before they heard your point.

They say about twenty percent (one in five) people will still answer a cold call. Virtually everyone still checks their voicemail, even if it's annoying.

Attention still exists. It just has standards now.

That's how we got here.

An entire generation decided cold calling is dead because they're bad at it and would rather hold a funeral for the channel than admit their opener has the seductive magnetism of a compliance webinar. Saying cold calling is dead because your calls suck is like saying dating is dead because your Hinge match replied "lmao" and never came back.

Nope. The app still works. The call still works.

You're the one making it weird.

Well, you, and a bit of AI.

Now everybody can produce poetic, competent, emotionally vacant nonsense at scale. Inboxes are flooded with messages that are technically correct and spiritually deceased. It's like speed dating in *Pluribus*, if every person had the same haircut, the same prompts, the same fake personality, and a suspicious interest in crypto. You match, engage, and three messages in, you realize you're talking to a script wearing a human skin suit.

Still, AI didn't kill outbound. Not completely.

It just made bad prospecting cheaper.

It did for outreach what ring lights did for bad opinions.

And the industry response to all this has been nothing short of inspiring, if your goal is to fail more efficiently.

Sales training today feels like bringing your mom to a nightclub. Maybe she was iconic once. Maybe in 2004 she really was outside, doing things with glitter eyeliner and low-rise jeans that changed lives. But right now she's standing next to the bar asking if this is "Justin Timberlake," and your soul is trying to leave your body through your knees.

That's how a lot of outbound advice lands on a modern buyer.

You've got people teaching cold calling who haven't carried quota in years, explaining neuroscience they don't use, and pushing permission-based openers that sound like someone asking if they even have consent to exist.

Red hat, red book, carnival barking might work in *Boiler Room*, but to real prospects, it just feels try-hard and gets you left on read.

"Can I steal thirty seconds?"

Nobody has ever heard that and thought, *"Please, sweep me off my feet."*

Some reps sound like emotional-support interns with a sequence tool.

"Just wanted to follow up."

"Bumping this to the top of your inbox."

"Circling back."

Congratulations. You're recycling the business version of "hey stranger."

You think prospecting should sound like getting hit on by someone who learned charisma from SaaS newsletters, and when that fizzles out, you assume the problem is wording.

It isn't.

It's the signal underneath it.

Old prospecting advice teaches you to lower your status before you've said anything useful. It trains you to essentially grovel for an outcome, and we wonder why that isn't "sexy."

Very few people, aside from a few outliers living mostly in Reddit forums (r/cringe), find neediness appealing.

No one cares how great your script is if you're already underneath reaching up.

You're already playing uphill in dress shoes on wet tile.

Everybody knows the smell of over-effort.

In dating, it smells like a paragraph of text.

In sales, it smells like "just checking in."

Oscar Wilde said it best:

"Everything in the world is about sex except sex, which is about power."

If that makes you squirm a little, good. It should.

Because this book isn't about sex. Or just about sales for that matter. It's about selection.

If you need the outcome, you lose control of the interaction. That's true in business, on a date, or in any room where the other person has options.

Desperation with better grammar is still desperation.

That's why scripts fail. They've got no presence, no intention, nothing beyond that painfully high-pitched undertone of *"please validate me."*

No clever line saves you after that, because your presence has had the same impact as a cold shower. It froze the mood, long before you had a chance to speak.

People love saying "I got rejected" because it sounds like they deserve to be watching rain trickle down a window while they listen to bad break-up music.

You weren't really rejected. You were skimmed and sorted into "Nope."

The market is not your mother.

Nobody owes you consideration just because you showed up.

I know that because I used to be exactly the kind of idiot who thought more effort would save me. I thought turning up the charm and treating every moment like a pitch competition was somehow attractive.

It isn't.

Effort isn't "Rizz". It's frantic. We can all sense when a date is going badly. One person is talking faster than an auctioneer, the other's already browsing their phone for the next match. Cold calling is no different.

Let me take you back through my own memory to a train platform in New Delhi.

Heat stuck to everything. Diesel in the air. Noise layered on noise until the whole place felt like one long mechanical exhale. People moving in every direction. No stillness. No center of gravity, really.

Then *her*.

She wasn't trying to stand out, so of course, she did.

You know that feeling when a room keeps moving, but your attention doesn't? Like the camera suddenly rack-focuses and the background drops out? That's what happened.

She looked at me once. That quick final look like the one Rue gives someone when she already knows how their story ends, and I knew immediately.

She'd already decided.

Not slowly. Not after hearing me out like a mature adult, comparing options, and checking Yelp reviews. Instantly. Pre-verbal. The same way you decide whether you're replying to a text before you've even fully read it.

It was over before I got a say.

We call that a chemistry clash because it sounds nicer.

It isn't chemistry.

It's selection.

And it happens before you get a turn.

As human beings, we hate that. We hate seeing the door closing, so we speed up.

More words. More effort. More explanation. More "Let me just say one thing." We try to justify our existence before the interaction has even had a chance to breathe.

Skip foreplay, then act shocked nobody's in the mood.

That's modern prospecting in one sentence.

Presence decides before words do. Once your presence sets the mood, words don't persuade. They *confirm.*

That's why some conversations feel easy, and others feel like dragging a boulder uphill while your manager yells "love the energy" in the background.

It's not what you said.

It's what *they felt* when you said it.

For a second on that train platform, I had the same reflex everybody has. Recover. Say something clever. Interrupt the decision. Rewrite the read before it hardens. Basically, do everything that would prompt her to reach for pepper spray.

The same reflex behind double-texting, overexplaining, and follow-up sequences that are really just anxiety in a nice CRM.

Seen. No reply.

Congrats. That's half the pipeline.

It's the panic that kills people. Reps think they're creating momentum, saving the moment. The other person feels chased. The interaction's already dead, and now you're just adding documentation.

Cold outreach isn't prospecting.

It's Hinge with a quota, and most of it reads like you already sent the second message.

That's the thing about neediness. It rarely feels like neediness from the inside. It feels like effort. Like doing what you're supposed to do to make something happen.

But effort at the wrong moment is just insecurity in business casual.

It's the professional version of a text you knew was a mistake while typing and still sent because what if this one "hits different?"

It never does.

I felt the urge to impress her. Then I let it pass.

Because anything I said to win her over would've confirmed the exact category she'd already put me in.

So I stepped forward and said the simplest true thing I had.

"You look stunning. I want to get to know you."

That was it.

No angle. No trick. Definitely no follow-up second sentence or quick joke like "unless you have a boyfriend, haha…"

I just gave the moment space.

She turned fully this time. Looked at me differently. Like maybe the interaction hadn't been filed away yet.

Then she asked, honestly, a pretty reasonable question:

"Why should I talk to you?"

It wasn't playful. It wasn't flirty. It wasn't even mean.

I could have started listing reasons, stacking value, selling myself, and explaining my personality like I was pitching for a wildcard slot on *Love Is Blind.*

That's how curiosity turns into evaluation, connection turns into an audition, and presence turns into performance.

And performance is replaceable. *Always.*

So I just repeated, "I'd like to get to know you."

For a second, silence.

Then she asked for my name.

Just like that, she stepped into the interaction rather than being pulled into it.

A few minutes later, she gave me her number. Not an "add me on Insta" request. A real phone number. Imagine that.

When she gave it, I said, "Only give me your number if you actually want to interact. Otherwise, I don't need it."

She nodded, and in that moment, I knew she'd chosen me. Not because I convinced her or wowed her with a great line, but because I didn't collapse.

If you think that story is about dating, you missed it.

It's about selection.

The same thing happens every time you send a message, make a call, or walk into a room where people have options. The decision happens before your first sentence lands. Everything after that just confirms the read.

You don't lose deals on the call.

You lose them before you say a word.

CHAPTER 1:

COLD CALLING: NO SPARK, NO ACCESS

"Power is in tearing human minds to pieces and putting them together again in new shapes of your own choosing."

– O'Brien

You dial someone you have no business reaching, and before you say a word, the sorting starts. Before you can pitch, the decision's made. You can start digging through the CRM and overanalyzing everything, because "DIFTP," right? But it doesn't matter.

They're already swiping left.

That's a cold call.

From the outside, it looks like a phone call. From the inside, it's more like crashing a scene that was already moving and never cast you. You're not the main character. You're not even the zany friend of the main character.

At best, you're a disruption. At worst, you're an ad with a pulse.

That's why so much cold-calling advice feels fake. It treats the call like a blank canvas when it's really a live filter.

The prospect already has a mood, a pace, a pattern, three other things happening, and no patience for somebody who sounds like they practiced this in front of a mirror. Your job isn't to "start a conversation."

Your job is to alter the temperature before the moment spits you out.

If nothing changes when you turn up, nothing starts.

No spark. No access.

The industry hates that truth because it makes half the training market look like arts and crafts for adults. So instead of dealing with reality, it keeps tweaking whatever feels controllable. More scripts. More talk tracks. More battle cards. More openers that sound like they were approved by Legal, HR, and a man who says "let's circle back" with his whole chest (and a bit of phlegm).

Then reps read them like actors in a rehearsal they almost believe in, no sense of self-awareness, no fire.

Everyone listening feels it. They hear the script they've heard five hundred times before, and they don't think, "They understood the assignment", they think, *"Great, another sales guy."*

The buyer isn't grading your opener for effort. They're reacting to your presence the same way you react to a voice note from somebody you already know is about to waste your time. You don't analyze. You feel, then you decide.

That's why cold calls fail so quietly. No one gets offended. They just "downvote" and move on.

You don't lose because you said the wrong thing. You lose because nothing about you made the moment, or the person, react.

Recognizable isn't safe. Recognizable is dead. It encourages a decision based on muscle memory while you're still standing there, mentally rehearsing what you're going to say in your best little quota voice.

That's why it's so frustrating that so many reps are still trying to sound "good" when they should be trying to sound alive. Slick copy now equals familiar and ignorable. AI made this worse. Every mediocre rep can now generate five versions of the same dead opener before breakfast and call it personalization, like ChatGPT can shape you into Don Draper.

The decision on a cold call happens before your insight, before your pitch, before your cute little note in Salesforce that says, "mention hiring push." It happens in that ugly-fast space where people feel first, explain later, and then call it logic because that sounds classier than "your vibe was off."

You have seconds to disrupt the pattern.

Patterns don't listen or evaluate. They either break or they continue without you.

The phone rings once. Halfway through the second, he picks up.

"Yeah."

That's it. One syllable. Flat. No warmth. No curiosity. The auditory equivalent of "k."

Not even an uppercase "K." The same "k" you'd deliver with the emotional range of someone declining cookies on a website.

You can hear movement behind him. Other voices. Keyboards clacking. Someone wrestling with a creaky door.

A whole life is already happening that has absolutely nothing to do with you.

The call can die in that moment, because nothing in the interaction gives the other person a reason to stay. It can die when you arrive like everyone else, composed, structured, desperately trying to sound both professional and polite, and say something lame:

"Did I catch you at a bad time?"

The line that should've been buried next to fax machines, overproduced Zoom backgrounds, and men who still say "circle back offline."

It's the perfect eject button.

Yes.

Click.

That response gets logged as timing, talked about later as activity, and almost never understood for what it actually was: self-sabotage.

"Did I catch you at a bad time?" is the cold-call version of "hey, sorry if this is weird…"

It tells on you immediately.

Because the brain doesn't process your words first, it processes your signal. And if your signal says, "I really need this to go well," the whole interaction tightens.

Need feels like pressure.

Pressure gets removed.

You see this everywhere once you stop pretending sales is some separate species of human behavior. Walk up to somebody with options and open with something a little rehearsed or approval-hungry, and watch how fast the air changes. They don't think, "*Wow, what a considerate communicator.*"

They feel the reach, and they sort you based on it.

That's cold calling. Faster. Cleaner. Less forgiving.

You're not starting a conversation. You're interrupting a pattern and seeing if the moment bends. That should change how you arrive. Do you show up like a person who belongs in the interaction? Or do you show up like you're asking for a small emotional grant from a stranger with a calendar?

I used to do the second one.

That's the humiliating part.

Old me heard, "I'm about to jump into something," and immediately started tap dancing. More words. Faster pace. More explanation. More "totally understand, real quick before you go…" I thought I was saving the moment. I was actually killing it in 4K.

That's what average reps do. They hear the distance and start lunging.

The better move is smaller. You don't introduce yourself like you're applying for a scholarship. You don't front-load your reason or start with respect-for-time nonsense.

You enter where their attention already lives.

"Who's owning your outbound right now?"

Nothing about that line is trying to *slay*. It's not trying to be cute. It's not trying to smuggle a pitch in under a fake question. It just starts in *their* world.

For a second, the pattern breaks.

"I am."

Flat. Controlled. Already halfway gone.

"…Look, I'm about to step into something."

There. That's the moment when you slow down and stop panicking.

Stay where you are.

"Got it. Then you'll know exactly why I'm calling."

That line doesn't chase or try to overpower the exit with charm. It just holds position.

There's a pause.

Then:

"…alright. Go."

That's it.

Not a meeting. Not a close. Just a continuation. That's the first win you need, because once the moment stays open, everything changes.

"You scaled the SDR team last quarter. Usually, that looks good for thirty days. Activity goes up, everyone feels sexy, and then reply quality starts slipping underneath it while the dashboard still looks fine."

Silence.

Then:

"...yeah."

There it is.

Now *that's* the kind of recognition you want.

"No one catches it early because top-line activity still looks healthy. Then pipeline quality splits underneath it, and by the time leadership feels it, the quarter's already messy."

A beat.

"Keep going."

Now you've got momentum. Not because you used the right framework or became ultra-convincing. Because you didn't feel like everybody else, like an interruption begging to be tolerated, you sounded like a person who noticed something real.

That's what access is.

People think the call is won when the meeting gets booked, when the calendar invite lands, when something measurable happens, they can screenshot and caption with "consistency compounds" like they're posting gym selfies for pipeline.

No.

The real win happened earlier. He gave you an exit, and you didn't run through it.

That's where cold calls are won and lost.

Because the second you reveal need, it doesn't just kill the spark.

It proves there never was one.

Step outside of "sales brain" for a minute.

This is *every* interaction that gets complicated because one side starts reaching and the other side leans back. Texting, dating, negotiations, interviews, group chats, every single human space where too much effort too early suddenly makes the whole thing feel gross.

People call that bad luck.

It's a signal response.

You feel pressure. The buyer hears need.

What you really need is less explanation, less performance, less effort, and more presence. When you signal pressure, you're coming across as effort. When you signal presence, you're acting like gravity.

Gravity pulls.

That's where older teachings tend to collapse. A lot of sales advice teaches you to aim for tolerance. Be respectful. Be deferential. Be grateful they even stayed on the line long enough to hear your little sentence.

You spend years following the same advice dished out in every performance improvement plan, and you still end up stuck in a rut. Because tolerance isn't "interest".

The moment you ask for tolerance, you're asking for permission to be heard, giving away your power, your leverage, and anything that makes you even mildly attractive.

ROUTE OPENER

You're not calling to pitch. You're calling to find the thread and *hopefully* grab hold of it. Give it a little tug. See what unravels.

A real route opener doesn't feel like you barged into somebody's day with a laminated value prop and an Instagram-worthy smile. It feels like you found the live wire in the room and touched it without blowing the place up.

A lot of reps I know still do the opposite. They blunder-call like they're crashing a conversation at a party, smiling too hard, trying to prove they belong before anybody notices they were there. It's the same energy as someone cutting into a group chat with "not to be annoying, but…" or sliding into DMs with "hope you don't mind me saying…"

It's *irritating*. So the whole moment tightens like someone forced into a badly fitted suit.

Realistically, you're not entering the moment "cold," even if no one recognizes your number. You're slipping into something that might already be in motion. A priority. A problem. A budget fight. Maybe even a political mess.

You can't sound like *another* interruption. You need to sound like someone who just happened to find the right door.

The goal isn't to "force" a moment. It's to locate one, then act like you're meant to be there.

A lot of reps think that means "prove value instantly." They start pitching in the first five seconds, which is the sales version of telling your life story on a first date, describing how many kids you want, and trying to plan out a wedding over breadsticks. Then you sit there wondering why the energy dies like a houseplant in a frat basement.

You've skipped context. You've skipped awareness.

Really, you've skipped the *basic social intelligence* that requires you to actually read the room and find out where the decision lives. So every call feels the same. Same setup. Same energy as a guy walking up to a stranger at a bar to say, "Come here often?"

You're not gaining access.

You're volunteering for humiliation.

A good route opener does less. That's why it works. You slow down before you speak. Ground yourself. Stop acting like something needs to happen immediately.

You don't prove value. You prove you belong.

So instead of opening with your company, your pitch, your "reason for the call," you start where attention already lives.

"Jasmin?"

"Yes, this is she."

"Hey, Abhinav Gokllani from Acme. Quick question. Who heads up your agentic AI strategy over there?"

Nothing's hiding inside that line. No fake curiosity. No pitch in a fake mustache. Just direction.

You're not asking to be tolerated, you're showing you're in the right place.

Then she says:

"I do. Why?"

And this is where reps think they've earned the mic, so they put on their best "main character energy" suit and launch into a TED Talk nobody asked for. Pace speeds up. Tone gets brighter. Words start stacking. They sound like a babbling pre-teen talking to their first crush.

Don't do that.

Stay where you are.

"I might have something in that area, but I don't want to waste your time. Does that decision roll up to you?"

That line qualifies authority and lowers pressure; something a lot of people struggle to do at the same time. They either qualify too hard and sound like an interrogator, or they lower the pressure so much they sound like they're apologizing for having a phone.

This just lets the answer reveal itself.

Same thing with "Hey, who owns the project management strategy at BNC Construction, beyond the IT team?"

That's routing.

You're not forcing the path. You're finding it.

If it's her, great. Continue.

If it's not, move on.

No apology. No tearful "totally understand" speech like you've just been friend-zoned.

"Got it. Who usually owns that?"

Wait for her to point you somewhere else. Then, when she does, don't reset the whole interaction like your GPS rerouted and now you're spiritually in the "upside down." Just extend the path naturally.

"Perfect. Would it be cool to mention you pointed me their way?"

That line does more work than countless full pitches. What started cold now carries context. What felt like an interruption now feels like a referral.

You didn't break in.

You got routed.

And once you're in, don't suddenly start break dancing because you think this is where you have to impress. Stay the same person. Same pace. Same emotional stability.

Same *lack of need.*

"Out of curiosity, what are you using right now?"

"Anthropic."

And now you're inside the conversation.

No pushing or dazzling the other party with Instagram filters. Just you, staying relaxed enough to let the route open itself.

TONALITY

A lot of reps hear "tonality" as *"more energy, more passion, more footwork…"*

Maybe they watched *The Wolf of Wall Street* once at a sales kickoff and never emotionally recovered. Now they sound like they're one chest pump away from trying to close a payroll software deal from a yacht.

That's just panic with bass.

Real tone is much less exciting than people want it to be. Calm. Measured. Unrattled. The kind of voice that doesn't sound like it's trying to make something happen.

That's the difference between bad and elite. It's not quiet versus loud. It's someone trying to be heard versus someone who already is. The amateur sounds like they need something good to happen before the caffeine burns off. The elite sounds like nothing has to happen at all, which is exactly why things start happening.

Calm isn't passive.

Calm is power without friction.

A pilot landing a plane doesn't sound excited. *Thank God.* He sounds certain. You don't want him sounding inspired. You want him sounding like this exact outcome was always the plan, and now everybody just needs to cooperate.

That's tonality.

Somewhere along the way, sales turned tone into performance. Like, if you just turned yourself up enough, people would lean in.

They won't. They lean away.

Because too much energy too early feels like pressure. It feels like a podcast host selling supplements. It feels like a man saying "my man" to strangers on LinkedIn.

In other words, it feels off.

And people are very, very good at hearing *off*.

Passion, too early, reads like need.

Need, no matter how well dressed, still reads like need.

That's why some reps sound technically good and still go nowhere. The words are fine. The timing is fine. The manager says, "Love the tone."

But underneath it all, the voice still says, *"Please let this work."*

That's what buyers hear.

Your tone is your nervous system on speakerphone. It's your internal state leaking through, whether you like it or not. If your whole aura is "need," whether it's the need for attention, attraction, or a sale, it comes across as desperation. Begging.

And buyers test this constantly. They pull back, get colder, shorten their answers. They throw friction into the call. Sometimes, just because they want to see whether you're about to start verbally windmilling the second they stop giving you easy energy.

You fail those tests the second your voice boa-constricts, your pace speeds up, and your pitch sounds like you're about to boil over. You come across like someone trying to negotiate their way back from being left on read.

That's why the strongest operators sound settled. Nothing to prove. Nothing to force. No urgency leaking out through the edges. No late-night DJ voice. No soft-launching confidence.

Fake confidence voice is gym-bro cologne. Strong at first. Overwhelming by minute two.

The strongest tone has almost no effort in it.

It just *continues.*

That's what makes it powerful. Stillness reads as control, and control reads as attractive.

If your voice starts chasing the moment, the moment starts typing "SOS" to its friends.

That's why I laugh when people say, "tone is everything."

No, it isn't.

You can deliver a terrible line in flawless tone, and it's still terrible.

"Want to see my meth lab?"

Perfectly calm. Great pacing. Warm baritone.

Still *awful.*

Tone doesn't fix the message. It reveals it.

So the goal isn't to engineer your tone like you're building a character.

The goal is to become somebody whose tone doesn't need engineering.

TAKEAWAY: PUT SOME DAMN HEAT INTO IT

On your next ten dials, stop opening like you need a hall pass.

Your opener shouldn't prove you were raised well. It should prove you belong in the moment long enough to create a spark.

People decide faster than you think. Faster than anything you can recover with a clever line later. You can't edge your way cautiously into that situation.

Too many reps still come in soft. Too polite. Too careful. "Oh, hey, sorry, can I just…chat for a minute…"

You can feel what happens on the other end almost instantly: tiny hesitation, slight pullback, the prospect not saying "No" yet, but immediately recognizing who's the cat and who's the mouse.

That's why "Did I catch you at a bad time?" is such a disaster. It sounds respectful. It actually works like an escape hatch.

Put it in a dating context, and it dies immediately: "Hey Jane, can I get thirty seconds to explain why you should go out with me?"

Exactly. *Who talks like that?*

No tension. No spark. No reason not to leave.

The other peak offenders loved by wrestler bros who think cocky equals funny are "This is a cold call, wanna roll the dice?" and "has my name been coming up over there?"

"Bro, this is pure cold, I don't know you from Adam."

This isn't Swingers, you're not in Vegas, and no self-respecting CFO is signing anything off that even if she fake laughs after hearing it for the seventh time today.

So change the entry. Start where their attention already lives.

"Who owns this right now?"

Now you're not asking for space. You're giving the moment somewhere real to go.

If you get friction, don't instantly turn into a man panic-texting out loud. Don't patch silence with extra words. Don't start sounding "friendlier" because the room chilled off. Lock in.

If they say, "I'm about to jump into something," try:

"Got it. Then you'll know exactly why I'm calling."

If they route you, let yourself get routed.

And stop restarting the interaction every time something shifts. You're extending the path naturally, not starting fresh.

Once you find your way into the moment, say one sharp thing.

One.

Not three stacked insights. Not a mini pitch wearing a cardboard costume. One observation they can recognize from their own world.

Then watch the room. Not the meeting booked. Not the calendar link. The room.

Did they slow down?

Did they give you more than they had to?

Did the tone shift?

Did they stop managing you and start engaging?

Movement is the first win.

A spark.

While you're doing all this, listen to your tone. Really listen.

Not just what you said, but what happened to your voice the second the call stopped going your way.

If your pace speeds up after friction, you're probably chasing.

If your pitch rises at the ends of sentences, you're probably asking for approval without realizing it.

If you start adding extra words, extra context, extra little friendly cushions, panic has entered the group chat.

If you can hear yourself trying to sound good, the performance has already started.

You want your tone to stay boring in the best way.

Steady.

Same pace before pushback and after it. Same shape when they're warm and when they're cold. Same emotional temperature when they say "interesting" and when they say "just send me an email."

That's composure. That's what people trust.

The goal isn't to sound confident.

It's to sound like the moment doesn't own you.

Find the spark, and let it burn.

I'll say this once, but it applies to every takeaway section in this book. Every practical prospecting skillset you could want is available on request: playbooks, call recordings, scripts, templates, sequences, frameworks. If you're stuck, that's on you. DM us anyway. We'll send exactly what you need.

CHAPTER 2:
OBJECTION HANDLING: DON'T FIGHT THE FRAME

Most reps hear an objection and react as if they've just been accused of a felony.

Suddenly, they're explaining, clarifying, defending, stacking reasons like they're trying to win custody of the conversation.

That's where it goes bad.

The objection is rarely the problem. Your reaction is.

An objection isn't a stop sign. It's usually a frame test.

The instant you treat it like something to fight, you lose twice. First, because now you're reacting, often as chaotically as Mentos dropped into Cola.

Second, because the other person can feel you trying to drag them back into a conversation they were already halfway out of. Force meeting force doesn't move anything forward.

It just makes the prospect want to disengage faster, usually in a way polite enough that you don't even realize the deal is dead until three follow-ups later, when you're "just checking in" with a corpse.

Stop pushing, start *redirecting.*

The first objection usually isn't a final decision. It's a reflex. A quick social defense to see whether you fold, flail, or start sounding like an unpaid defense attorney.

Don't answer the objection. Answer the frame underneath it.

It helps to sort what you're hearing.

Reflex objections are things like:

"Not interested."

"Send me info."

"I'm busy."

Those are often automatic. Fast. Protective.

Constraint objections are things like:

"No budget."

"Wrong timing."

"Procurement will block this."

"We already have a vendor."

Those may be real, but they still need context.

Take "We don't have a budget."

Some reps hear that and start arguing about economics like they're trying to save a town hall. ROI, cost savings, business case, urgency. All of it poured out too early because they think intensity creates belief.

It doesn't.

The second you argue the budget, you accept the budget as the frame, and now you're trapped inside their excuse.

A cleaner move is this:

"That's usually what people say right before they decide it's worth finding. What kind of return would make this a priority?"

Now the conversation isn't about whether money exists. It's about what would make the money move.

You're not debating a constraint. You're exposing a condition.

Same with:

"Send me information."

On the surface, that sounds cooperative. In reality, it's the corporate version of "we should totally hang out sometime." Everybody knows what's happening.

Weak reps hear that and react like they've been handed a second chance at life. Deck sent. PDF attached. Follow-up queued.

Amazing.

Now the deal gets to die slowly instead of honestly.

"Send me information" is where mediocre deals go to be taxidermied.

So instead of complying immediately, be real.

"That usually means no, right?"

Or:

"Be honest, does that mean you want info, or does that mean you want me to go away politely?"

That makes the conversation human again. No aggression. No weird edge. Just enough honesty to interrupt the script. Once the script breaks, something real can happen.

That's the part most reps are too scared to find out. They'd rather keep the interaction technically alive than actually know where they stand.

It's Schrödinger's pipeline: neither alive nor dead, and somehow still on next week's forecast call.

Then there's:

"I don't take cold calls."

Many reps either apologize or justify themselves. Both are terrible. An apology says you have something to apologize for. Justification makes you sound rattled.

Try this instead:

"Wait, then what does your sales team do?"

That line doesn't argue. It tilts the frame. It's a raised eyebrow, not a fistfight. You're not trying to overpower them. You're making the statement bump into reality.

Same with:

"I'm not interested."

A lot of the time, that's a reflex said too early. So answer the truth underneath it.

"You decided that before I spoke."

Delivered calmly, that lands. Not because it's clever. Because it's accurate.

And then there's the classic:

"We already have a vendor."

Good. Most companies do.

Weak reps hear that and instantly turn into jealous side pieces. They start trying to discredit the vendor, manufacture dissatisfaction, or force a breakup that nobody asked for. That creates threat, and threat creates defense.

Defense kills momentum.

A stronger move is:

"Totally get that. Why not plug us in alongside them and multiply what's already working?"

Now you've removed the threat. Your vibe is confidence and trust, not begging. You're not trying to replace what exists on day one. You're expanding what's already there, and expansion is much easier to accept than disruption, especially early.

That's what objections really are. Not walls, just moments where the interaction can either suffocate or keep breathing, depending on how badly you need to win right there.

You don't need to overpower the objection.

You need to stop treating it like the end of the story.

BOUNDARIES, PRONOIA & ANTIFRAGILITY

There's a line between persistence and thirst.

A lot of reps pole-vault over it. Then they act shocked when the whole interaction starts feeling creepy.

Boundaries are what keep persistence attractive.

That's the job here. Not rules for the sake of rules or corporate-etiquette cosplay. Just standards that stop your outreach from turning into digital desperation in a slick fit.

No personal email because the work address ignored you. No random FaceTime, like the building's on fire and only you know where the extinguisher is.

Definitely no back-to-back calls like "???" but with dial tone.

All of that has the same energy: trying the locked door, then the side gate, then the kitchen window, then pretending you were just being resourceful.

Outreach in a trench coat.

The moment outreach feels like a pursuit, your leverage dies. Most reps create pressure and call it urgency. They think more force equals more seriousness.

It doesn't. Force creates recoil.

Nobody looks at the fifty messages you sent when they were trying to ghost you and thinks, "Wow, confident."

They think, *"Who raised you?"*

Same with channel-switching. If there's real rapport, yes, move to text. Move to WhatsApp. Move wherever the conversation naturally wants to live.

But it has to feel like a continuation, not a workaround, because email ignored you and now you're trying to sneak through a side entrance.

Sending a message to their personal email because work didn't land has big found-your-finsta energy. *Creepy.*

I've had moments where I wanted to send the extra email, try the personal address, hit one more channel, just to feel like I was still in it.

Every time I've done that, the energy got cheaper. I wasn't *serving* anyone anymore; I was hounding them like a persistent ex five minutes away from getting a restraining order.

Bad persistence doesn't just fail. It lowers your position while it fails. It feels less like omnichannel outreach, more like the opening scene of a true crime podcast.

Show some self-control.

If someone says they don't want to talk to you, stop talking. Immediately. No last angle. No "just before I let you go." No "totally understand, one quick thing." No little final Hail Mary because somebody on LinkedIn said *persistence wins.*

Nothing reads stronger than restraint that doesn't need to be explained.

A lot of reps still confuse activity with composure. They leave a voicemail every single time because they want to feel like something happened. They hit another channel. They keep touching the sequence as if body heat is the only way to keep the moment alive.

That's not a strategy. It's closer to stalking.

Boundaries keep your discomfort from becoming the other person's problem. You don't get extra points for making someone uncomfortable in four channels instead of one.

If you think about it, this whole chapter is about self-respect in motion. Can you handle a little objection without breaking down? Can you stay present without chasing? Can you follow through without lunging? Can you leave room without disappearing?

That's calibration.

And calibration isn't aggression. It's control. It's the difference between somebody who's steering the interaction and somebody who's frantically trying to grab the wheel after already drifting into a hedge.

Too much pressure, too early, and the door doesn't just stay closed. It slams into your face. At that point, the next knock lands differently. Imagine running towards a cat at full speed and expecting it to just wait for you. *Yeah, right.*

That's where pronoia really helps. Not pronoia as in fake positivity, or "everything happens for a reason" in cross stitch. Just a different mindset: the market will cooperate with you if you *unclench* for a second.

Two reps can run the same playbook and get completely different outcomes because one of them is carrying emotional residue like a browser with 47 tabs open, and two of them are playing audio.

The last bad call leaks into the next one. A rejection sticks. A hang-up lingers. An objection gets under your skin. Now the next conversation is contaminated.

You're contaminated.

And contaminated reps do wild things. They rush. Push. Over-explain. They give out the uncomfortable vibe of an addict desperate for their next hit.

That's why the better reps are cleaner. They're not dragging messy ghosts into the next room. They get out of the moment, touch grass, and reset before poisoning the next interaction.

Once you stop clinging to every bad moment like an ex's hoodie you refuse to throw out, things get lighter. You stop protecting your ego, and you build something sturdier.

That's the antifragility part of all this.

Some reps try to avoid bad calls. Others just try to survive them.

The dangerous ones use them.

Every awkward pause, objection, hang-up, and tonality shift is useful. Every ugly little moment sharpens pattern recognition if you let it.

That's how you stop reacting and start anticipating. You hear hesitation before it hardens into an objection. You feel timing before it becomes a miss. You can tell when someone is actually busy and when they're just trying to see if you collapse.

The system refines because the environment is noisy, not in spite of it.

That's the point.

The goal isn't to protect confidence.

The goal is to build something that doesn't depend on confidence at all.

TAKEAWAY: DON'T GET WEIRD WHEN THE ENERGY CHANGES

On your next ten calls, stop treating objections like you just got punched in public.

When you hear the slightest resistance, don't suddenly transform into the younger, needier, frightened version of yourself. You shouldn't be explaining like a guy caught liking his ex's vacation photos at 1:12 a.m. It's too much, too fast, and way too revealing.

That's how objections win. You react to them as if you're facing the end of civilization.

So start there.

When someone pushes back, don't ask, "How do I overcome this?" Ask, "What are they actually protecting right now?" Because the majority of first objections aren't deep truths delivered from the mountaintop. They're reflexes.

That means your first job isn't to fight the objection.

It's not to embarrass yourself in response to it.

If they say, "I'm busy," and you immediately start sprinting through your pitch like you're trying to beat the Oscars music, you lost. If they say, "Send me information," and you react like you've been chosen by the sorting hat, deck attached, case study loaded, follow-up scheduled, you lost.

If they say, "We already have a vendor," and you instantly start trashing the vendor like a jealous Tinder match, you've *definitely* lost.

So on your next calls, watch for your tells.

Do you speed up? Get brighter? Add extra words? Try to sound more reasonable?

Calm down.

Change the frame instead.

"No budget" becomes:

"What kind of return would make this a priority?"

"Send me information" becomes:

"That usually means no, right?"

"I don't take cold calls" becomes:

"Wait, then what does your sales team do?"

You're not trying to become verbally unbeatable. You're trying to make the conversation more honest. That's what good objection handling really is. Not a rebuttal contest. Not a little UFC match in business casual. Just staying steady.

The same thing goes for persistence.

Bad persistence often feels justified. It feels like being proactive. It feels like "just covering all my bases." And then suddenly you're three channels deep, one personal email away from being screenshotted in somebody's internal Slack like a cautionary tale.

So watch yourself there, too.

If they don't reply, do you immediately send something else just to feel less invisible? If a call goes badly, does the next call get your leftover frustration? If one prospect ghosts you, do you re-cast your personality for the next five?

That's what needs fixing.

Not your template. Not your sequence.

Your state.

The clean reps reset fast. They don't drag one ugly call into the next like emotional carry-on luggage. They hang up, clear it, and move. No internal monologue. No "why does this always happen to me?"

The previous call gets no custody rights over the next one.

You move forward, and you keep your standards while doing it. You listen to the objections without letting them destroy you. You respect the boundaries. And above all else, you stop catastrophizing everything.

You're going to get bad calls. That's the job.

The better question is: what did that one teach me before the dial tone finished dying?

That's how the craft evolves.

Not by staying protected.

By staying observant.

CHAPTER 3:
VOICEMAIL, POLARITY & RUNNING THE CALL

A lot of reps want to be memorable without being present enough to register.

That's not how memory works.

A single call, a single email, a single voicemail, then disappearing for four days like you got drafted into another war, that doesn't make you memorable. It just proves you own a phone and an email signature.

Presence works differently.

It imprints. It becomes familiar. Not in a forced way. In a human way. Like a song you heard on the radio and now know all the words to.

Frequency doesn't have to equal pressure. Sometimes it can feel like a pattern. A rhythm.

Memory likes rhythm.

Buyers do too.

I once called a COO twenty-five times over a few months. That sounds *wild* if you've learned to treat rejection like a personal boundary violation instead of part of the job.

But when he finally picked up, there was no frustration in his voice. No "bro, enough!" energy.

He said, "Hey, Abhi."

Relaxed. Familiar. Like we were old friends.

We had booked once, and he had to reschedule. But the bigger thing was this: repetition didn't push him away. It made me part of his environment.

Then he told me something.

He listens to his voicemail every day because he wants people to know he's available.

Every rep who didn't leave one never existed to him.

That's where you really start walking the tightrope between boundaries and persistence. Because cyberstalking isn't sexy, but backing out of the room completely because you're afraid of being "too much" isn't going to close the deal either.

One voicemail won't make you memorable. It just confirms you know how phones work.

But a sequence? That's different.

Bad sequencing feels like panic dished out in installments.

Good sequencing feels like coordinated presence.

Familiarity lowers resistance long before it earns trust. Repetition, in the right direction, builds recognition, tension, and even attraction. It's not "Duolingo owl threatening your family" familiar, just familiar enough that your name stops feeling like an interruption.

And if you understand that, your sequence changes.

You stop operating in isolated little attempts, each one emotionally loaded, each one treated like a fresh shot at destiny.

Instead, you stack. Call. Voicemail. Email. Tight window. Not random. Not dripped out like a confused situationship. Coordinated.

I remember when a CEO of a billion-dollar construction company hung up on me. He was busy. A lot of reps would log that, tell themselves it was bad timing, maybe send a "following up on our brief conversation" email, and disappear into the CRM mist.

I called him back.

"You were busy last time, and you already told us we're the best in the business. Is now a better time to talk?"

He booked the meeting.

Why? Because the energy didn't reset. There was no apology, hesitation, or fresh start; just continuation.

That's the thing. Reps might treat every touch like episode one. The prospect doesn't.

If they've seen your name, heard your voice, watched you show up consistently, you're not cold in the same way. You're a pattern, and those are easier to trust than strangers.

That's why voicemail plus email works so well when it's tight.

Here's the clean version:

- Voicemail under 20 seconds if you can
- One idea only
- No callback ask
- Email lands right after
- Same thread, same energy, same motion

Voicemail:

Hey John, Abhi from Acme, (805) 723-0063. I have a product that's very relevant to your work. Beta Corp justified this with a one percent reduction in security costs, about $30M annually, saving roughly $30K a year. I've got an idea to improve your setup. If it's relevant, great. If not, I'd be curious what didn't land. Again, Abhi from Acme, (805) 723-0063. I'll follow up with a note.

Then the email hits right after.

Subject: per my voicemail

John,

Beta Corp justified this with a one percent reduction in security costs, usually hitting around $30m per year, which worked out to roughly $30K a year.

Worth pressure-testing that against your world for thirteen minutes?

Case study here: [link]

– Abhi

That feels connected.

You're not asking for a callback like you're going to be refreshing WhatsApp at 2:15 am. That's just handing the prospect another to-do list.

You're continuing the motion.

And yes, you should leave more than one voicemail in a real sequence. Four to five across a sequence is fine if the touches are clean and the gaps make sense.

Not because one needs to land. Because your name needs to feel known, one touch says, "I was here." A sequence says, "I keep showing up, and I don't sound rattled doing it."

That's what starts to feel like credibility.

I've had weeks where I got five connects and booked five meetings. Not because I suddenly became the chosen one. Because the touches were coordinated, the tonality stayed clean, and I didn't vanish after the first little sign of resistance.

That's the standard. If your touches feel random, they feel needy. If they feel coordinated, they feel intentional.

That's the difference between spam and signal.

POLARITY SHIFTING

A polarity shift is the moment the interaction flips, and nobody announces it.

At first, they're evaluating you. Fast. Impatient. Half out the door. You can hear it in the clipped answers, the guarded tone, the little defensive questions that are really just a polished way of saying, "Why are you here and how fast can I make this end?"

Then something changes, and they're the ones leaning in.

Early on, "What are you selling?" lands like a shield. Quick. Dismissive. Functional. It's not curiosity. It's *pest control.*

Later, after they've been talking, after you've let them expand without pouncing on the first problem they mention, the same curiosity comes back wearing different clothes.

"Wait, who are you with again?"

Totally different energy.

That's not defense anymore.

Polarity flips when curiosity changes sides.

You see it everywhere once you know what to look for.

In calls, dates, meetings, and parties. Any room where attention isn't free and everybody's pretending they're less interested than they are. At first, they're scanning, sorting, deciding whether you're worth another second. Then, if you don't ruin it, they start pulling you back in.

Trouble is, a lot of reps get that little hint of curiosity and immediately punish it. They become unbearably informative. More words. More shine. More "value."

Suddenly, they sound like a contestant on *Love Is Blind* who got one good pod date and lost all motor control.

As soon as they lean in, your ego becomes the problem.

The first thirty seconds to two minutes aren't for proving yourself, unloading insight, or doing a tiny product demo with your voice.

They're for shaping the air.

That means questions clean enough to land and sharp enough to open something real.

"How are you thinking about pipeline coverage going into this quarter?"

That starts in their world, not yours.

"It's decent, but conversion's been off."

And this is where a lot of reps internally black out.

They hear a problem and instantly want to solve it. Diagnose it. Show they're smart. Show they've seen this before. Basically, wave their arms around yelling, "Pick me, I know the answer!"

Stay still.

"Where does it tend to break?"

Now you're not solving. You're expanding.

"Mid funnel."

"Has that been building or did it hit all at once?"

That's what good sellers do. They add dimension without adding pressure. Every answer pulls the buyer deeper into their own thinking, which is where real engagement actually comes from.

"Yeah, it's been building."

And then it happens.

"Wait, *who are you with again?*"

That's the moment where attention changes hands.

Now they're *interested.*

When that happens, don't fumble like it's your first kiss and you've only ever practiced on your hand. Resist the urge to throw out features, decks, proof points, and too much tongue. That's how you talk yourself out of the room you just got invited into.

Do less.

"I work with revenue teams on that gap."

That's just enough to anchor the moment without crowding it.

Then, if the moment's right, you make your move. Lean in.

"Let's take twenty minutes and actually look at it. What does your calendar look like this week?"

No hedging, "would you be open to…"

No soft little ask that sounds like you need permission to keep existing.

Because once the polarity shifts, your job isn't to prove you're interesting. For now, you are.

Your job is to move the moment forward without breaking it.

RUNNING THE CALL: THE DANCE OF CONTROL

Once the polarity shifts, don't ruin it by celebrating too early.

Many reps do. The room leans in, and the rep responds with an essay and a praying hands emoji.

Running the call is what happens after access. You're not worried about getting in anymore; you're keeping the conversation alive once it's already breathing.

A weak rep treats the call like combat. Block, counter, pitch, objection, rebuttal, next slide, fake laugh, survive. KO. It's all force. Fast hands. Bruce Lee in a nice shirt. Like they're trying to ride a mechanical bull while explaining product architecture.

A strong rep does something simpler. They step into the space with a clear intention. They're there to guide, not wrestle the moment into submission.

That's why RRM works. Not because it's a script, but because it respects how movement actually happens.

Three gates.

Route. Ruin. Multiply.

It works in sequence, like the Panama Canal. You don't skip a gate. Clear one, and the next opens naturally.

Most reps treat calls like kickboxing. RRM is closer to Brazilian Jiu-Jitsu: less force, better timing, cleaner leverage.

That's the dance.

ROUTE

Route comes first because orientation beats persuasion.

You are not opening the call to "learn more about their business." You're opening to locate where the truth lives and who's carrying it.

That's why the first move needs to be clean.

"Who owns API management on your side?"

"Who's closest to pipeline quality right now?"

"Who's handling this day to day?"

Simple. Direct. Easy to answer.

No speech. No throat-clearing. No little "for context" paragraph trying to prove you were raised right. You're there to get oriented.

They answer.

You validate lightly.

"Got it."

Then keep moving.

Route isn't where you prove value. It's where you establish that this conversation has shape.

A bad opener has substitute-teacher energy. A good opener feels like you found the right door and opened it without making the room stop and stare.

RUIN

This is the best part, and it's where reps tend to panic.

You've got the person. They're talking. There's air in the room. Then, insecure sellers start attacking the current vendor, forcing urgency, or trying to sound smart enough to matter.

All terrible.

Ruin does the opposite.

You begin with what they already use.

"What are you using right now?"

They tell you.

"Oh, they're great."

That line disarms, lowers threat, signals maturity, and tells them you're not here to make them defend a decision they already made. Nobody expects that much emotional stability from a seller.

Then you open the hinge.

Not "why are they failing you?"

Just:

"How's that working out for you?"

Now they start talking like a person instead of a position.

Then you follow the thread.

"What do you like about it?"

"When did you put that in?"

"What else did you look at?"

Here, the listen-to-talk ratio flips naturally. You're not trying to hit 80/20 because some manager put it on a slide once. They just start talking because you're not crowding them. And the more they talk, the more the real thing shows up.

Trade-offs, workarounds, political compromises, tiny frustrations they've normalized because no one's asked them to actually look at them bundled together.

That's the red thread.

You're not "asking good questions." You're tightening one thread until the person can see the shape of the thing they've been tolerating.

A doctor doesn't need twenty random symptoms. They need the one pattern connecting them. A good therapist doesn't react to every sentence. They hear what keeps repeating underneath them. A great call works the same way.

You're not collecting facts. You're finding the tax.

That's the real job of Ruin. Not to create pain, but to surface cost.

Ruin is basically *The Traitors* for vendor language. You're listening for what they're trying *not to say.*

And once they hear themselves say it clearly, the call changes.

Not because you "handled the objection" or "built urgency."

Because the problem stopped being ambient and became visible.

MULTIPLY

Now comes the third gate.

The point where weak sellers accidentally trigger fear.

Because the second a problem becomes clear, the buyer starts doing math they will never say out loud. How hard is this going to be? How political is this going to be? How much existing stuff gets threatened? How embarrassing is it to admit this setup isn't working as well as we said it was?

That's the real resistance.

Fear of change.

So, don't threaten the current system. Remove the cost of movement.

That's Multiply.

"No need to replace anything. We just plug in and multiply what's already working."

You're not asking them to rip out a system they fought to get approved, like they're banning their old boyfriend from their Netflix account. You're not asking for a spiritual reset disguised as implementation. You are making the yes *additive.*

And additive is easy. It's also less painful.

Nobody wants to publicly admit they bought the wrong thing in Q3. Nobody wants to sponsor a massive transition if they can avoid it. Absolutely nobody wants to create chaos just to prove they were open-minded.

So don't sell replacement too early.

Sell leverage. Sell amplification. Sell less friction, more output, more signal, less manual pain, less internal tax.

That's Multiply.

Put together, it sounds like this:

"Who owns API management on your side?"

"Got it."

"What are you using today?"

"Oh, they're great. How's that working out for you?"

"Makes sense. What else do you wish it could do?"

"Who ends up dealing with that?"

"No need to change anything. We just plug in and multiply what's already there."

That's a call that *does something.*

WHAT THE FIRST CALL IS ACTUALLY FOR

The first call is never where you "win."

That's fantasy. That's rom-com sales logic. One perfect line, music swells, meeting booked, everybody claps, somebody posts about grit with a GIF of Shia LaBeouf.

No.

The first call doesn't win the deal. It decides whether the deal *deserves* oxygen.

Did you find something real enough to keep alive? Did the thread lock in? Did the room change? Did stillness start to feel costly?

If yes, the next step makes sense.

If no, no amount of "great conversation today" email energy is going to revive it.

That's why running the call matters so much, because calls don't die from a dramatic mistake. They die from drift; too much explanation, too little shape, no thread, no consequence, no movement.

A call that moves doesn't feel loud. It feels directional, more F1 pit wall than podcast alpha: calm inputs, tight timing, no unnecessary wheel-spin.

That's what people trust: the person who can move the conversation one clean step at a time without making the room feel handled.

That's the dance. Push too hard, and you kill it like Disco. Hang back too much, and the moment disappears. But if you guide it with the right amount of pressure, the next step stops feeling like a close and starts feeling like where the conversation was always headed.

That's the trick.

People don't move because you dazzled them.

They move because staying where they are starts to feel unfinished.

TAKEAWAY: PUT IT INTO MOTION

On your next call, use structure instead of improvising yourself into a mess.

Start with Route. Get oriented quickly. Ask who owns it, who feels it, and what the setup is. Keep it clean and easy to answer.

The goal is to get the conversation pointed in the right direction.

Once they name the current setup, don't create a threat too early. Validate first. Keep them from defending the status quo before you even know where it bends.

Then move into Ruin by finding the tax: where it strains, where it gets manual, who owns the mess, what happens if it keeps going.

If they finally say something real, stay there long enough for it to sharpen.

Then Multiply.

Don't make the next move sound like a painful reinvention.

Make it sound additive, lower-friction, easier to say yes to.

If the thread is real, the next step should feel like a continuation, not a dramatic scene change.

The same rule applies to voicemail and sequencing. Don't treat each touch like a separate emotional event. Treat them like connected signals.

Your voicemail should leave one idea behind. Your email should continue the motion, not restart the story. Your sequence should feel coordinated enough to be remembered, but clean enough not to feel like a pursuit.

Watch for the polarity shift without throwing a parade the second it happens. At first, they're managing you. Then, if the room changes, they start adding context, asking another question, or circling back on their own. When that happens, don't suddenly become more excited than the situation deserves. Anchor it, then move it forward.

A few simple checks help:

- If you're talking more than they are by minute three, fix it.
- If you attack the current solution too early, expect defense.
- If you hear something useful or painful and glide past it, that's on you.
- If the next step feels abrupt, you rushed it.
- If the conversation feels like it naturally wanted another layer, you probably ran it well.

And this logic travels.

Interviews work the same way. Don't walk in trying to answer correctly like you're sitting an exam in a nice blazer. Take direction early. Shape the room. Ask what separates the people who thrive from the people who stall. Make it feel like a live working session, not a recital.

Promotion works the same way, too. Titles rarely move because you did your current job slightly better and waited politely. They move because your conversations start sounding like someone already operating at the next level.

That's the standard.

Not more performance.

More direction, more thread, better timing. More cowbell.

CHAPTER 4:

COLD EMAIL: HE SAW IT. HE FELT NOTHING. HE MOVED ON

"The reasonable woman adapts herself to the world. The unreasonable one persists in trying to adapt the world to herself."

– George Bernard Shaw

The inbox isn't reading you.

It's sorting you. Not in a friendly way, either.

Nobody is opening your email and settling in with tea and a highlighter.

They're scanning it mid-thought, mid-scroll, mid-chaos, with six other things already fighting for attention and a brain that has become frighteningly good at deciding, within seconds, whether *this* deserves another breath.

That's why cold emails fail when they're boringly, aggressively familiar.

The structure gives itself away too fast. The intent shows up too early. The whole thing feels repetitive by line two, and once that happens, the brain closes the loop and moves on.

Automatically.

The same way you skip a Hinge profile that somehow managed to say nothing in three prompts and two professional headshots.

A finished email is so easy to ignore. It tells you too much, resolves too much, and leaves the reader with nothing to do but hit "delete."

Completion kills tension. Tension is what holds attention.

And attention is the only thing you're actually trying to earn here, at least, at first.

You're not there to present information. You're there to intersect with something already alive on their side. A friction, double, wrong assumption. Maybe a problem they haven't named yet. If your message meets that correctly, it doesn't feel like an interruption.

It feels like relevance. Understanding.

That's what survives.

Something unresolved.

The trouble is, leaving something unresolved requires restraint. We're not taught to act that way. We're brainwashed into believing that more explanation equals more value, so a lot of cold emails show up dressed for the Met Gala and somehow still have the sex appeal of printer toner.

I understood this in a moment that had nothing to do with email and *everything* to do with attention.

San Diego Union Station. Middle of the day. Everybody moving with that low-grade urgency people perform when they want the world to know they have places to be. Phones out. Eyes down. Energy fragmented. And across the platform, there's someone who clearly isn't participating in any of it.

I spotted her.

Most people would either ignore that moment or force it.

Both fail.

So instead, I stayed where I was, opened my laptop, angled it just enough to be seen without throwing out "main character" vibes, and wrote:

"You look like you opted out of whatever this place thinks it is."

No pressure. Nothing trying to define what should happen next. Just enough specificity to feel real and enough space to stay open.

She glanced over. Paused. Smiled in that way people do when something lands slightly outside the expected pattern. Then she stood up and walked over.

What made that work wasn't the line.

It was that it didn't *feel like one.*

If it had felt familiar, like something she could instantly categorize, it would have been less appealing than pouring ice on her back.

That's the mechanism in cold email, too.

Not better wording or smarter frameworks.

Avoid recognition long enough for attention to stay.

MESSAGING & COPY: THE MOMENT YOU TRY TOO HARD, IT'S ALREADY OVER

There's a very specific kind of modern insanity where a message gets written like it's auditioning for Harvard, McKinsey, and a situationship all at once, and still gets ignored faster than a doomed Netflix reboot.

That's the joke.

Nobody's really losing because they "can't write."

They're losing because they write like they want to be selected by professionalism itself.

Every sentence arrives overcooked. Over-parented. Over-explained. Like it's about to be judged by the ghost of Steve Jobs, Don Draper, and one emotionally unstable RevOps manager who says "tighten the copy" like a parrot hoping for a cracker.

Some outbound messages sound like they moisturize.

And the reader, whether it's a CRO, a founder, or somebody deciding if you're worth replying to after 11:47 p.m., does the same thing every time.

They skim once, feel everything too early, and leave.

That's the collapse point. Not bad writing.

Over-completion. Over-explaining. Over-trying.

The moment you make it too easy to understand, you also make it too easy to *dismiss*.

People hate hearing that because they think clarity is the flex. Being understood is proof of value. *Nope*. Attention doesn't behave like a polite student taking notes in class. Attention behaves like a spoiled celebrity with a five-second clip tolerance and no loyalty to your effort.

If the moment doesn't feel like it's going somewhere slightly dangerous, slightly unresolved, slightly not finished, attention skips out.

That's true in email copy, in DMs, and in dating. It's true anywhere desire and attention share a hallway.

You see it everywhere now. LinkedIn messages that sound like a committee of anxious therapists approved them. Cold emails written with the energy of "I'm trying very hard not to offend the idea of rejection." DMs that feel like someone trying to pitch low-pressure authenticity.

And underneath all of it is the same mistake.

They think saying everything cleanly increases response.

Usually, it just completes the experience for the other person, so they don't have to *do anything*.

That's what messaging gets wrong. The brain doesn't reward completion; it archives it and moves on. The only thing the brain responds to is tension.

That tiny psychological itch that says, "*Hey, this isn't finished yet.*"

That's why the most effective line in an inbox is the one that refuses to resolve anything.

One example I saw was when I was watching a CRO clear his inbox. Messages vanished almost as quickly as they appeared. Polite. Structured. Recognizable. Gone. Then one slowed him down.

"You might be solving the wrong problem."

That was all it said, and that was enough.

That CRO didn't respond immediately. He did something better.

He read it again.

That second look is everything. The first skim is algorithm, the second look is desire sneaking past security.

The trouble is that high-effort communicators kill their own best work. They find one sharp insight and then bury it under three layers of context, two layers of credibility signaling, and one unnecessary apology for being in the prospect's inbox at all.

By the time the actual idea shows up, attention has already gone back to NBA highlights, TikTok, Slack, or whatever completely unserious theory the internet currently has about celebrity breakups and the meltdown of civilization.

Now the tension's gone. *Unsubscribe.*

This happens in dating all the time, too, which is why it's so funny watching people pretend sales is different. Somebody sends a slightly bold message, then instantly follows up with "haha… Hope that didn't come off weird."

Translation: "Please ignore the only interesting thing I just did."

You walk into the room like Kanye, then apologize for having legs.

So many messages end up feeling like they were written by a smart person trying to sound safe enough for procurement and sexy enough for pipeline. *Tragic combo.*

Attention doesn't wait for your setup.

It doesn't *owe* you patience.

It only moves toward what feels unfinished.

That's why a single line can beat a full paragraph.

Because it has less closure.

It behaves like a door left slightly open in a house you were never supposed to enter. Now your brain's doing all the work the message refused to do for you.

And once that happens, the dynamic changes.

You're no longer chasing attention.

You're holding it.

That's the same mechanism that makes someone replay a scene in *Euphoria* because one line felt colder than it should have. Or why the person on a dating app who says almost nothing somehow occupies more mental real estate than the ones writing paragraphs about communication, their four-legged "children," and "good vibes."

The human system rewards anticipation.

That's why the most dangerous communicators are the ones who know exactly where to stop.

"You're probably focusing on the wrong thing."

That line doesn't ask for agreement or permission. It doesn't even fully explain itself. It just dangles in the air like a housefly waiting for someone to reach out and swat it.

As soon as they lift their hand, they're not consuming a message anymore.

They're participating in it.

They're trying to resolve it.

That's the leverage point.

And that's where messaging stops being just "writing" and starts controlling where the mind goes next.

Most people never get there because they keep optimizing for clarity, when clarity is often the exit ramp.

Clear is useful.

Complete is forgettable. Easy to archive, and easy to discard.

That's especially true in high-noise environments where the brain is looking for any excuse to move on.

A call gives you room to recover. A message doesn't.

On a call, tone can buy you another ten seconds. In copy, once they've filed you as ignorable, it's over.

That's why some of the best messages have a light *Black Mirror* quality.

Almost unsettling.

That's what gets them screenshot and forwarded in Slack threads with "WTF, is this actually true?" written under them. It's what gets them replayed in someone's head at 1:13 a.m. when they've finally stopped scrolling Reddit.

The first job of copy isn't to get understood.

It's to earn the reread.

PATTERN INTERRUPTS: PREDICTABLE ISN'T ATTRACTIVE

"Be yourself. Everyone else is already taken."

– Oscar Wilde

Normal is the most dangerous aesthetic on earth.

Normal can be dismissed without friction.

It's the same feeling as opening Netflix and seeing another true-crime documentary with a grayscale thumbnail, a woman whispering over piano music, and a title like *Buried Secrets of Maple Creek*. Maybe it's good. Maybe it isn't. Doesn't matter.

Your brain already knows what category to put it in, which means the decision is basically made before the trailer even loads.

That's what most outreach feels like now.

Pre-solved.

And once something feels pre-solved, attention leaves before meaning gets a chance to do anything useful.

People today think they're competing with other messages.

They aren't.

They're competing with pattern recognition.

The brain doesn't read first. It sorts.

That matters more than almost anything else in outbound, because people love pretending the problem is their copy, their CTA, their "relevance," their send time, or the phase of the moon. The real problem is simpler: The message got recognized too quickly.

Seller. Spam.

Outreach. Template.

"Loved your post." "Congrats on the growth." "Quick question for you." "Saw your recent funding round." *Delete later.*

That's it.

The sorting happens instantly.

And the faster it happens, the less your message matters.

That's why familiarity isn't safe, or comforting; it's invisible.

The moment something feels like it belongs in a category people are trained to ignore, you're *done.* Not rejected, or disliked. Just mentally filed under "I know what this is" and compressed into the wallpaper.

That's the real humiliation.

You didn't lose because they hated your prose. You lost because they barely had to *experience it.*

A lot of modern outreach can be technically "good" and still hit this hurdle. You did the research, personalized the opener, mentioned the "gem" you were told to mention, and maybe even congratulated the buyer on their promotion as if you were the only human on LinkedIn who noticed the platform set off confetti.

And still, nothing.

You didn't earn attention; you acted *exactly as expected.*

That's why the usual excuses are so dishonest. People say inboxes are crowded, buyers are impossible, nobody reads anymore, attention spans are dead, and AI ruined everything.

No, you're just far too easy to categorize, right alongside all the LinkedIn creators using the same "honest" tone like they're auditioning to be the internet's most emotionally available VP of Revenue. Next to founders quoting Naval like it counts as a worldview.

Even on top of dating profiles saying "love food, travel, and not taking life too seriously," which is just a scenic way of saying *I am exactly like everyone else, but with better Lightroom presets and one picture on a boat.*

At some point, everything becomes optimized into sameness.

Look at everyday outbound. Someone finds a line that works, a format that works, a tone that works, and then within six weeks the whole market is doing karaoke with it. Suddenly, everybody's "human," everybody's lowercase, everybody's a little uncertain, everybody's "not sure if this is relevant but…"

Even an anti-pattern has become a pattern.

Pattern interrupts are a lifeline when predictability is fatal.

The point isn't to be louder. To be funnier. Or to act like a LinkedIn performance artist who discovered caffeine and irony on the same morning.

The point is to arrive just outside the category.

People hear "pattern interrupt" and think chaos. Wild opener. Random humor. Forced originality. A subject line that sounds like a nervous breakdown. Outreach in a wacky tie.

That's just being annoying in a more memorable outfit.

A bad pattern interrupt doesn't break the category.

It just becomes irritating in a slightly different font.

You're not trying to confuse anyone; you're just trying to delay automatic classification.

No chaos. No "I'm so quirky" vibe. Just misalignment without distrust. Something *off enough* that the brain can't finish the pattern instantly, but still grounded enough that it doesn't feel manipulative, bizarre, or thirsty in a creative-writing way.

All you need is a pause. A moment where the system that usually deletes you has to stay open one beat longer than it wanted to.

That's why the best messages are rarely the ones that sound the smartest. They're the ones that break their own category before the category closes around them.

They're not try-hard funny, just unexpectedly real. Just far enough outside the box.

Think anti-lines like:

"I might be completely off here."

"This is either irrelevant or useful, not sure which yet."

"I should probably not be in your inbox."

"Can I ask you a slightly bizarre question?" (Crack for DM responses)

"This might be noise, but…"

Those are effective because they interrupt the usual sorting process. They remove the polished certainty that normally signals, "A seller is about to do seller things to me."

And people have seen that movie enough times already.

So when the message opens with something that doesn't feel fully locked into the usual category, the brain wakes up a little.

Because it can't finish the script yet.

That's the opening.

Not your proof points.

Not the paragraph you're dying to add because you're scared the message might look too simple, and your internal committee of fake professionalism is panicking.

Completion soothes the sender and kills the message.

Then there's personalization.

A lot of reps are so proud of personalization because they think it proves they've put in the effort. That's not really true anymore. Anyone can say "Congrats on your Series B" after a quick check on LinkedIn. It takes relevance to say: "You probably have a VP right now trying to look in control while the org grows faster than the process."

Huge difference.

One notices a fact.

The other notices pressure.

And pressure is what makes things move.

That's also why overly polished certainty often works against you. In a market full of AI slop, fake confidence is embarrassing. Everyone is certain now. Everyone is "excited to connect." Everyone "works with teams like yours."

That's why uncertainty, used correctly, works so well.

Not weak uncertainty. Not apologizing for existing.

Clean uncertainty.

"Could be wrong."

That doesn't lower your position. It actually protects it, because it signals that you're not forcing a narrative. You're observing something and offering it lightly.

Paradoxically, that makes it harder to ignore.

Everyone else sounds certain in a way that feels like marketing.

You sound attentive in a way that feels like thought.

That's what keeps the message alive long enough to matter.

Then you go in with Hyper-P, but only if you understand what it is. Hyper-personalization isn't more data. It's not scraping the internet until you know what conference somebody attended in 2019, where they got their MBA, and what they said on a panel no one watched.

That's digital stalking with decent UI.

Hyper-P, when it works, is perception, actual relevance, noticing the thing ChatGPT would tag as "too human to matter."

Your prospect can tell the difference between "this was assembled from profile fields" and "someone actually clocked me."

The first one reads like a "This is your life from the last two weeks" update your phone generates from your camera reel. The second one shows you've done the work.

Next time you want to personalize something, don't add more "bullet points" of things you've noticed. Build a mini business case.

"Could be wrong, but based on the last three posts your CTO shared on LinkedIn, your job listing for a new AI engineer, and the fact that you completed a funding round last month, it looks like you're working on a new app. You might be focusing on the wrong things first."

A message like that is calm; it shows you're paying attention, and it leaves something incomplete. That's why it hits different.

You aren't trying to "grab attention." That phrase has awful energy. It sounds like a man with a clicker, a ring light, and a six-part content series on thought leadership that scales.

You're trying to prevent automatic dismissal.

That's a much cleaner game.

TAKEAWAY: PUT IT INTO THE INBOX WITHOUT KILLING IT

Before you send anything, stop asking, "Is this good?"

Ask something meaner: "Have they seen this before?"

If the theme announces itself in line one, the message is already halfway to the trash.

Openers like "hope you're well" suck. The brain already knows which genre they belong to, and it's not interested in sitting through another episode.

What works better is language that interrupts sorting without turning into performance art. Things like:

- this might be off…
- this might be a weird read…
- not sure this is relevant, but…
- saw something that made me think of your Q2 push…

Those lines don't "convince." They buy another beat of attention.

After that, keep the body narrow. One idea. One observation. One pressure point.

"Saw you just hired a new CTO from ACME Corp. They've done a lot of work with AI lately. If you're going to be taking that route, there's a common mistake you should know about."

No stack of insights, no long runway, no paragraph trying to prove you're thoughtful, strategic, humble, and easy to work with all at once, like a LinkedIn dating profile for procurement.

A useful check is this: if the message sounds like it could go to fifty people, rewrite it. If the "personalization" is just public trivia, cut it. If the message feels polished enough for leadership review, loosen it. If it sounds clever in a way that wants applause, simplify it.

If it creates a small pause before understanding, you're probably closer.

Don't kill the only living line in your email by over-explaining it. The extra sentence you add, "just so they get it," is usually the one that ruins it. Same energy as spoiling the ending or explaining the joke like a psychopath. A sharp line turns into a paragraph, the paragraph into a brochure, and suddenly it smells like a webinar with a Slack channel.

The follow-up should stay in the same frame, too. Don't suddenly change tone, reboot the thread, or act more excited just because silence made your nerves start filing internal complaints. A short continuation usually works better than a full restart:

- thoughts?
- am i off here?
- worth pressure-testing?
- curious if this is real on your side or just noise

Short helps because it feels like a continuation, not a fresh little campaign in a blazer.

If you want surface variation, fine. A short email, a screenshot, a quick voice note, a one-line re-entry. But the goal isn't randomness. It's to avoid becoming instantly fileable.

And the award for the cleanest breakup email ever goes to?

"Can you have the courtesy to point me to who handles this?"

Ignoring that shows zero courtesy, and that's not a good look.

CHAPTER 5:

SOCIAL SELLING: THEY ALREADY KNOW IF THEY WANT YOU

"We see things not as they are, but as we are."

– Anaïs Nin

There's a certain kind of person who thinks if they just post more, explain more, and repackage the same thought twelve different ways with slightly better lighting and a "hot take" hook, eventually something will tip in their favor.

As if attention is a punch card.

As if LinkedIn is quietly keeping score and, after ten spicy carousels and one vulnerable post about leadership, the market hands you a free latte and a pipeline.

That'd be nice.

It's not reality.

Because being seen was never the same as *being chosen*.

Everybody knows this. Same way, everybody knows within seconds whether they're interested in someone before that person has "*a chance to explain themselves*." Logic always shows up late, hair slicked back, pretending it made the call. It didn't. The body did. The pattern did. The vibe did.

That's social selling, too.

People don't slowly reason their way into wanting to talk to you. They either feel something immediately and lean into it, or they keep scrolling.

Visibility doesn't create interest if the thing being made visible already reads as ignorable. No one sees another Tinder profile featuring a copy-paste "would love a good chat" bio and a picture of a guy in sunglasses doing *Blue Steel* and thinks, "*finally, mystery.*"

More exposure to someone who already filtered you doesn't help.

It's just digital haunting.

The business version of posting thirst traps for people who already muted you.

That's why so much social selling looks active and feels dead.

The posts are there. The comments. The soulless emojis. The little "great insight" drive-bys written with all the warmth of a receipt printer. But nothing's actually happening.

Because people on LinkedIn aren't building trust.

They're rehearsing relevance in public.

LinkedIn, especially, is an odd room. Everyone says it's a professional network. It's really *The White Lotus* with job titles. Everybody's smiling, networking, and pretending to be relaxed. Somebody's still getting cut out of the deal.

Reps ruin social selling by trying too hard too early. They get one inch of engagement and immediately start capitalizing on it like they just got called up from the minors. More context. Pitch. Relevance. More "would love to share what we're seeing in this space."

Same mistake people make in *Euphoria*. One flicker of attention and suddenly they're acting like the moment owes them something.

Now the whole thing has *Love Island* confessional energy. Too much confidence. Not enough self-awareness.

The moment something starts forming, they manage it to death.

Because social selling isn't really about posting; it's about pace.

It's whether you can feel when an interaction is opening and resist the urge to turn it into a funnel. That's rarer than people think. A lot of what gets called social selling is just public thirst in better lighting. Portrait-mode illumination with bullet points. A content strategy with abandonment issues.

Real movement looks different.

It's smaller. Usually more human and less impressive. A reply that runs longer than it had to. Maybe a question coming back instead of a polite close. Something that feels unfinished but worth pursuing.

If you feel interest and immediately start performing, you kill it.

You turn chemistry into paperwork.

Being interesting on social doesn't come from saying more. It comes from leaving something alive long enough for the other person to step into it.

That requires restraint, which most people don't have because every platform rewards instant output and constant resolution. Say the thing. Post the lesson. Add the CTA. Make the clip. Keep it moving. Everyone's acting like the algorithm is their emotionally unavailable ex, and maybe this next post will finally make it care.

Real attention needs a little room.

The best social interactions work the way *Challengers* works. Tension first. Explanation later. Nobody ruins it by stepping into frame and narrating the dynamic while the dynamic is still doing its job.

That's why the people who are actually good at this aren't just clever, they're *more aware.*

They notice what's forming, and they don't interrupt it.

They leave just enough unsaid that the other person has to complete it.

And once the other person completes it, even a little, the dynamic changes. It stops being you presenting and them evaluating. Now it's shared. Co-created. A real exchange instead of content rubbing against a stranger and calling it nurture.

By the time your name shows up, they've already guessed what category you belong to. The only shot you have is to interrupt that guess before it hardens.

Not with the kind of performative cleverness that screams, "I drafted this three times and still think it sounds casual."

With something that doesn't resolve immediately.

Something that makes them pause for half a beat and think, "*Okay, wait.*"

All you need is curiosity.

But curiosity is fragile.

The second you try to monetize it too aggressively, it dies.

That's why social selling works best when it doesn't feel like selling yet. You need something real to happen before you drag process into the room.

That feels like continuity.

It's the difference between "Hi, nice to meet you" on Tinder, and "Hey, I noticed your pic from Italy, do you spend a lot of time around Sorrento?" One invites the conversation to keep going, the other invites it to disappear.

DM FLOWS

DMs are the new cold call. You're not messaging. You're tapping the infinite money glitch. *Unlimited meetings unlocked.*

You're not starting anything. You're stepping into something that was already moving without you. Same with every call, every email, every dating app thread.

That's why so many DMs feel pushy the second they land. The person on the other end already has a mood, a pace, a hundred tiny assumptions, and almost no patience for someone arriving like a networking intern with a template and a dream. Most LinkedIn outreach has that exact energy. Like somebody cutting into a group conversation at a party just to say, "Hey guys, super random..." and then immediately sharing a bad idea.

A lot of reps slide into DMs like they're wearing a lanyard at a party.

That's the first problem.

People treat LinkedIn like email because email feels safer. More polished, more complete, more professional. More little sentences designed to prove you were raised right. But chat doesn't reward completeness.

It punishes it even more than email.

The more finished your message feels, the easier it is to ignore. Same reason a perfectly wrapped pitch makes people want to reject it on principle. It feels like work. It feels like somebody is about to *need something from you.*

Or worse, it feels like chatting to a bot.

That's why what actually works usually looks a little undercooked at first. Not sloppy. Not lazy. Just alive. Sent, not assembled. Like it came from a person with pulse and timing, not a company trying to soft-launch sincerity.

"Loved your recent post" is basically the corporate version of "hey, haha."

Once a message feels generatable, it becomes disposable.

So you go one layer deeper. Not like you're mining their profile for a personality loophole. Just enough that the message couldn't have been copied and pasted onto ten other people before lunch.

Mention something odd.

Something specific.

Something they chose to leave visible that most people were too busy driving engagement to notice.

You were a champion rabbit breeder.

You competed in a cappella.

You dropped an Enneagram reference on LinkedIn and survived.

Those lines don't feel like outreach. It feels like you actually *saw something*, which is rarer than it should be on a platform full of people rehearsing relevance in public.

And sometimes even that's too much.

Sometimes the cleanest entry is the one that barely explains itself at all.

Blank connect. Then:

"what's your big vision for 2026?"

Lowercase. No setup. No "hope you're well." No little runway to prove you're thoughtful, strategic, emotionally intelligent, and easy to work with.

It doesn't feel like something they're supposed to respond to.

It feels like something they *could* respond to.

Big difference.

The moment a message feels optional, it gets more interesting.

You're not trying to impress them.

You're giving them something that doesn't immediately close.

That's the entire game.

Because once there are two or three exchanges, something changes that most people miss while they're still trying to drive the conversation.

You're no longer an outbound message.

You're inside something.

And once you're inside, direction can't show up like a hard pivot. It can't feel like the software demo just entered the chat wearing business-casual cologne. It has to feel like continuity. It has to emerge like a good scene in *Euphoria*. You almost don't know what's happening until you're shoulders-deep in the moment.

"this might be easier to show than explain, open to a quick zoom?"

No spike in energy. No sudden shift into sales mode. No weird transformation where your work-self takes possession of your body and starts talking like an off-brand prestige-TV executive. Same tone. Same pace. Same thread. Just slightly more defined.

The moment it feels like a pivot, it gets treated like one.

If it feels like a continuation, people stay.

Everything on the other person's profile exists because they chose for it to be seen. You aren't hacking your way in. You're stepping through a door they already left open. Most people miss that because they're too busy trying to build a new entrance and impress themselves with how creative they are.

If it's on the profile, it's fair game.

You're not invading.

You're noticing.

And curiosity does most of the lifting from there. Not pressure, urgency, or fake scarcity. Not whatever testosterone-and-tripod content taught a generation of sales bros about closing.

You're not pushing.

You're stepping in, letting the moment breathe, and only pulling when it's already moving in that direction.

That's how conversations become calls.

And this is the part people secretly don't like because it forces them to admit the obvious.

This isn't really prospecting.

It's flirting with job titles.

Same rules. Same mistakes. Same over-explaining, over-positioning, over-performing that kills attraction in every other room too.

The moment you try to prove your value, you lower it.

I used to get a good reply and immediately ruin it by becoming useful too fast. More context. More polish. More "helpfulness." Basically, taking something alive and turning it into admin.

Old me would've gotten the reply I wanted and answered like I was pitching at a conference.

That's how you turn tension into homework.

Now I know that.

Most people don't need better DM scripts.

They need to stop sounding like someone desperate to get a reply.

TAKEAWAY: GET SOCIAL, NOT CREEPY

Don't try to build attraction with administration.

That's what a lot of social selling turns into. More posts. More comments. More DMs. More "thought leadership." More effort with the emotional texture of an airport Marriott. Then people wonder why the market saw it, felt nothing, and kept walking.

So start smaller.

Pick fewer people. Not prospects. People.

People you'd actually want to talk to if you were stuck next to them at a wedding, at an offsite, or in line for absurdly expensive coffee while pretending rent isn't a hate crime.

Spend a minute in their world like a normal person. Not scanning for keywords like you're robbing a résumé. Not doing FBI cosplay in their activity feed. Just noticing something specific.

That's where the message starts.

Not with "Loved your recent post." Nobody believes that anymore. That line has the same energy as "hope this finds you well" and "quick question for you." Technically legal, spiritually expired.

A better opener feels noticed, not deployed. Something like:

- saw the move from Berlin to London while scaling SDR. that's a lot at once.
- you made that sound calmer than I'm guessing it actually was.

- random question - what's been harder there than people think?
- you still think that's the real bottleneck?

That's enough.

If they reply, don't suddenly become strategic. Don't hit them with a paragraph. Stay in the rhythm that got the reply. Keep your side shorter than theirs for as long as possible. The second you start over-explaining, it stops feeling like chat and starts feeling like customer service with ambition.

Better follow-ons sound like:

- makes sense
- yeah, that's usually where it gets weird
- what changed first?
- was that obvious right away, or did it sneak up on you?

Now watch for the actual signal. Not just whether they replied, but whether they started giving you more than they had to. More detail. More honesty. A second question. A little complaint. That's when the DM stops being outreach and starts being a conversation.

Only then do you give it shape.

Not a hard pivot. Not "part of the reason I reached out…" while the room is still warming up and your sales breath is already fogging the windows. Keep it in the same world:

- we've been seeing that exact mess show up a lot lately
- there's a version of that we've helped clean up without adding more complexity
- might be easier to show than type if it's relevant

Then, if it still feels warm:

- up for a quick Zoom?
- worth exploring?

- easier to walk through live if useful
- give me 11 mins or pass?

That last one works because it doesn't sound like you built a shrine to the meeting.

And don't make the practical mistake people always make with social: assuming more content equals more pull. Posting more can help distribution.

It doesn't automatically create magnetism.

That's why social selling is less about volume than recognition and pace. The first job is to not sound like somebody who rehearsed this in Notes and then asked ChatGPT to make it warmer. The second job is not to ruin the thing once it starts.

Good DMs feel like FaceTime energy.

Bad DMs feel like a calendar invite learning to flirt.

CHAPTER 6:

VIDEO & VISUAL PROSPECTING: IF THEY DON'T FEEL YOU INSTANTLY, IT'S OVER

"To be seen is to be known."

– *Michel Foucault*

You thought video was going to save you.

Finally, a chance to be more human. More personal. More you. Better lighting, cleaner framing, a little *Euphoria* glow, and suddenly prospects will feel your sincerity through the screen and book meetings out of pure emotional alignment.

What actually happens is much less flattering.

Video doesn't give you more control. It removes the control you thought you had. Text lets you curate. You could trim, smooth, revise, and become the slightly more composed version of yourself. Video takes that away and drops you into the room with no edit, no distance, no strategic little rewrite after the fact.

That's why video is so unforgiving. It doesn't reveal your message first.

It reveals your state.

Before they process your point, they've already processed your pacing, your eyes, your breath, the way you're sitting, the slight strain in your voice, the tiny signal that says whether you're sharing something or trying to make something happen.

The decision gets made fast. The same way attraction gets read fast. Not step by step. Not logically. All at once. Like a glance that lingers half a second too long. Like someone turning back after they already started to leave. Like that tiny involuntary shift where attention stops being given politely and starts being given voluntarily.

You don't explain your way into that.

You either carry it or you don't.

And most people don't, which is why so many prospecting videos feel technically fine and spiritually doomed.

You've seen them. Maybe you've made them. Clean frame, decent audio, structured delivery, nice smile. Everything in place. And still something is off. Nothing obvious enough to criticize. Just enough that your thumb starts looking for somewhere else to be.

It feels like effort.

And effort, on camera, reads badly.

Visible effort in a first-touch video feels like need. Like trying to impress someone at the gym with your "sick gains". Like someone on a date saying all the right things while making the whole table feel like an interview.

The more the production value increases, the more "pressure" there is to show off. You go back to being pretentious, not conversational.

A lot of reps feel the awkwardness like a slap in the face when they watch the video back. Then they make it worse.

They tighten up, refine more, and rehearse more. They do one more take, fix the lighting, rewrite the opener. Try to make it cleaner, sharper, and more professional.

They slowly sand off the last human part of it and end up with a video that looks like a rejected audition for a startup keynote.

What they don't get is there's a beauty in being *scrappy*. Being real. Like when someone answers your question of "how's it going?" with "pretty crappy, actually." You pay attention.

It's not what you expected, but it's *authentic*.

Some reps hit record and immediately become the most unnatural version of themselves, like a stand-in news anchor trying to act casual while visibly reading off a teleprompter in his bloodstream. You're no Ron Burgundy.

The problem is never your wording. It's what's sitting *underneath*.

I watched a founder stumble directly into this without realizing it. Same audience. Same offer. Same basic point. The first version was flawless in all the ways that don't matter. Good camera. Good structure. Nice little arc. Rehearsed enough to feel polished. And underneath it, you could feel the tension. That desperate need for it to land.

It didn't bomb.

It just went *thud*.

Watch time fell off early. Replies stayed vague. Interest never turned into movement. It had all the right parts and none of the gravity.

The second version changed almost nothing on the surface and everything underneath. No script. No real smoothing. He just hit record while the thought was still alive and said it before his inner consultant woke up and started asking for revisions. He left a little air around the words. Didn't rush to fill the silence. Didn't try to "bring the viewer along." Didn't sound like he was hoping to be chosen.

Watch time doubled. Replies got more specific. Meetings showed up warmer, like people were stepping into something instead of being pushed toward it.

The dynamic changed, not the wording.

That's why it worked.

Video success isn't about saying better things. It's about removing the part of you that's obviously trying to make the thing work. Because in video, that "effort" is painfully noticeable.

And once it's felt, the interaction tilts away from you in the subtlest possible way.

Attention starts slipping without friction. Like someone checking their phone while you're still technically talking. Like a scene that looked promising and somehow never pulled you in.

The moment that need disappears, everything reorganizes on its own. Your pacing slows, your tone settles, and you stop reaching for the next line like you're trying to beat a buzzer. You stop acting like the silence is an emergency.

And in that space, attention shows up because it isn't something you add.

It's something you *stop interfering with.*

You see it in tiny moments. The pause you don't rush. The silence you don't patch. The sentence you don't over-explain. The thought you let land without stapling a lesson to it.

That's when attention starts moving toward you instead of away from you.

That's when the interaction stops feeling like a pitch and starts feeling like a pull.

This is where video becomes more than delivery.

It becomes exposure.

Every frame is saying something before your words matter. The way you sit. The way you look into the camera. The way your face changes when you get to the point you care about. Whether you seem calm inside your own body or like your nervous system is trying to host a webinar.

All of it gets read instantly.

The same way confidence gets read across a room without anyone consciously knowing what they're noticing.

You can't manufacture that in real time.

You can only stop disrupting it.

And when it's there, even briefly, the dynamic opens. A simple clip holds longer than it should. A single idea lands deeper than it normally would. Not because it's extraordinary. Because it feels grounded in something that isn't asking for anything in return.

Raw doesn't mean sloppy.

It means alive.

There's a difference between unforced and underprepared. One feels present. The other feels like you recorded this while looking for your AirPods.

Where this starts compounding is in sequence.

Not everything at once. Not one perfect video carrying the whole relationship on its back like a doomed reboot. A short clip that catches attention. A simple visual that sharpens it. A message that leaves room instead of forcing closure. Each piece nudges things forward without pressure. The same way attraction builds when nobody's narrating it to death.

That's the part that matters.

Not the structure. Not the script. Not even the angle of your camera or the size of the subtitles.

The absence of anything in you that needs it to work.

That's what makes people tune in.

OSCAR-CALIBER VIDEO

Video is the most intimate channel you have.

Which is exactly why people ruin it the second they hit record.

They take what should feel like a passing moment and turn it into an audition tape for a role nobody asked them to play. Somewhere between a corporate training video and a startup explainer with excellent lighting and absolutely no sex appeal.

Bad prospecting video feels like a rejected YouTube pre-roll ad with eye contact.

Or hostage footage for a seed round.

Or a startup pastor trying to be casual.

You are already inside their DMs. That's rare. That's intimate. That's a weird amount of access if you really think about it. And instead of respecting that, most people overproduce it like they're making a mini launch asset.

Better camera. Cleaner audio. Nicer framing. Sharper intro.

All of which usually makes the whole thing worse.

Because a polished video raises suspicion.

It's like seeing an overly perfect picture on Instagram where the caption screams #nofilter, but the person's face miraculously doesn't have a single pore or blemish. It's like listening to your not-sodedicated partner tell you *"you're the only one for me, baby"* in a way that sounds like they've said the same thing five times that day.

Real video collapses that distance because it feels like something happening, not something built. The brain always leans toward what feels alive over what feels constructed. That's why a slightly imperfect clip shot on a phone often lands harder than something that looks like it belongs on a landing page.

Video at this level isn't performance. It's presence under observation.

And presence can't be faked without becoming obvious.

That's why you record it inside the LinkedIn app, on your phone, maybe in motion, maybe in a coffee shop where something tiny is happening in the background that you didn't control. Those imperfections signal this is happening now.

Ditch the beige wall and bookcase flex. Mash up rough cut "wow moment" product fly-throughs in iMovie. Be like JP in Spain, turning hikes with his celebrity collie into dog-led growth.

You still think before you speak. But not so long that the thought dies.

Then you keep it simple in a way that feels almost too simple if you're used to trying.

"Carol, I realize I'm sliding into your DMs, but we're working with a few teams like yours right now, helping them reduce stack complexity and clean up forecasting without adding pressure on reps. Had a couple of thoughts for your team. If it's relevant, I can share. If not, I'd actually be curious what didn't land."

The reason that works is the same reason someone who doesn't over-explain themselves is more interesting to be around.

You aren't trying to convert.

You are creating a moment that stays open. Slightly unfinished. A little unresolved. Because unresolved things pull attention forward in a way that completed thoughts never do.

That's the overlap between sales and seduction nobody likes admitting, and everybody responds to anyway.

And this is where people miss the real leverage.

When nothing comes back, they assume the move is to try harder.

It usually isn't.

The real move is to do less in a way that feels like more.

If the first video gets nothing, don't escalate.

Soften.

You send a second video that doesn't improve the message. It releases the pressure underneath it.

"I guess I'm not winning an Oscar for that one. Where'd I lose you?"

That line resets the room.

Humor plus self-awareness is lethal. It snaps you out of pitch mode and back into being a person without asking for permission.

That second touch lands because it removes the invisible weight that made the first one easy to ignore.

Want replies? Ask for a blunt take.

"Thick skin. What did you actually think of that?"

Karen mode activated.

That's the move.

Asking for an opinion is the fastest way to get a meeting on any channel.

Pressure kills curiosity every time. Curiosity is the only thing you're earning here, whether you admit it or not.

You're not chasing.

You're leaving the door open.

And when the door feels open, people step through it like it was their idea.

Vampires cannot cross the threshold without an invitation.

VENNTASTIC GIFS

You aren't sending messages.

You're staging momentum.

People keep missing that.

They still treat outreach like each message has to do all the work by itself, like every touch is a first date, a breakup, and a closing call all at once. So the first message over-explains. The second one gets needy. The third one shows up in a different tone, as if it suffered a personality event between sends.

That's not a sequence.

The sequence is *the effect.*

Not the wording. Not the copy. Not the clever line you underlined in your own draft and got too attached to.

The way it unfolds. The way it pulls. The way each touch does less on the surface and more underneath. The way it changes how you're experienced without ever announcing that it's doing it.

Three touches are usually enough.

And if you do it right, each one gets lighter.

The first touch lands clean. Under fifty words. A one to three-word subject line, or just their name in lowercase, "the most beautiful sound in the human language." Nothing that signals preparation. Nothing that feels like you've thought about this longer than they have. The second it feels constructed, it feels like effort.

So the first touch doesn't close.

It opens.

Just enough that ignoring it feels like a decision.

Then touch two is almost nothing.

This is where most reps absolutely disgrace themselves. They panic because the first touch didn't get immediate love, so now they "add value," which is usually just a respectable way of saying they discovered anxiety as a strategy. More context. More explanation. More detail. More little sentences trying to prove this was worth reading the first time.

Touch two should feel like eye contact, not a rebuttal.

"thoughts?"

That's it.

No rewrite. No buildup. No, "wanted to follow up on the note below." That line has killed more attraction than bad breath.

Then touch three changes the medium.

That's when the dynamic changes.

Because visuals land before the brain has time to decline politely.

Your brain locks onto visuals in about 13 milliseconds and remembers roughly 65 percent of them days later, while text barely holds 10 percent.

Which is why peacocks go full neon and the best-dressed guy in the club already won before he says a word. Meanwhile, the industry is out here writing creepy over-personalized ChatGPT prompts like a digital stalker and wondering why someone with real presence just walks in and takes the deal.

Pattern break beats personalization.

Personalization is expected now. It's getting your email system to add someone's name to an empty field in the subject line and acting like that's chemistry.

Pattern break is what stops the scroll long enough for thought to happen.

That's where most people reach for something polished and kill it. They make it pretty, branded, and professional. In other words, they go "extra."

Now it feels like a deck. Or marketing. Or like you just discovered Canva.

A good visual doesn't decorate your point. It makes the right thing obvious faster.

One rough diagram.

One overlap.

One asymmetry.

One before-and-after.

One scribbled tension map that mirrors the reality they're already living in but haven't named yet. That hits harder than a paragraph because it removes the need to convince. It shows instead of arguing.

It reveals instead of persuading.

That's why the highest-leverage version is usually yours. Not stock. Not polished. Not some smug little illustration from a design system. *Yours.*

Make GIFS.

Take the strongest moment from a demo. The exact second when a buyer leans in. The moment a dashboard changes shape. The point where something becomes obvious without needing a sermon under it. Then clip that moment into a short loop.

No context paragraph, trying to hold its hand like an over-eager romantic on a first date.

Just the moment.

That's what the GIF is for.

Not "look what our product does."

More like: "look at the exact instant this stopped being abstract."

A good GIF should feel more like a reaction clip than a product brochure having a panic attack.

Then the Venn.

Three circles. One overlap. One gray area. Slightly unfinished. Slightly cryptic. Like a thought caught midstream before somebody in RevOps could ask for a cleaner legend and branded colors.

You're not trying to impress them.

You're trying to make their brain participate.

By touch three, if the sequence is working, you're not trying to earn interest. You're already inside the moment. The dynamic's changed. They aren't just receiving. They're participating. Leaning in. Extending the moment without being asked.

That's when the sequence stops being something you send and starts being something they don't want to drop.

Not because you pushed harder.

Because you never needed to.

TAKEAWAY: LIGHTS, CAMERA, ACTION

Stop treating video and visuals like mini campaigns and start treating them like real human moments.

For video, keep it native whenever you can. Inside LinkedIn. Inside the DM. On your phone. In the actual place, they're going to consume it.

Asking for one extra click is often enough to kill the moment.

Keep it under thirty seconds, not because some hyperactive growth goblin on LinkedIn said "sub-30 is king," but because longer videos start sounding like you need to be understood. The second you start trying to be understood too hard, you often stop being felt.

Then, pick a few people you'd genuinely want to talk to. Spend a minute on each profile like a person, not a crawler. What changed? What's under pressure? What looks stable on the surface and slightly chaotic underneath? Then record once, before your brain turns it into a keynote.

Say one thing. One observed pressure. One open door.

Something like:

- saw you're expanding SDR into EMEA. That's usually where quality starts slipping while volume still looks fine. Curious what you're seeing on your side.
- looks like you're scaling without changing much process. That combo usually gets expensive quickly.

- you may already have this covered, but this is often where forecasting starts getting weird.

That's enough.

If you want a follow-up video, don't come back louder. Loosen the room instead. The Oscar touch works because it releases pressure:

- i guess I'm not winning an Oscar for that one. Curious where I lost you.
- not exactly Cannes material. Still curious if this is noise or real on your side.
- That may have been aggressively mediocre. open to telling me if I'm off?

They work because they're vulnerable without feeling needy. Letting prospects coach you is bold AF.

For visuals, think compression, not decoration. The job isn't to impress. It's to make the right thing obvious faster. A rough Venn. A single chart. A before and after. A messy flow where quality breaks as volume scales. These work because they pull the reader in. If they have to think, you're cooked.

In enterprise sales, there's a twist. Confusion, used deliberately, can create curiosity.

We once sent a crop circle to the Fortune 1000. It opened 80 opportunities.

But most of the time, complexity kills momentum. Silence isn't neutral.

"What is not overtly positive is covertly negative."

– Brian Burns

"I loved our date so much I disappeared for three weeks to process it."

Maybe they're busy. Or maybe you got quietly archived.

That's not a great look.

That's why a simple three-touch flow beats a full content opera.

Touch one:

- saw you're adding reps while opening a new segment. That combo usually breaks quality before anyone admits it.

Touch two:

- thoughts?

Touch three:

- a simple before/after pipeline GIF
- or a messy Venn: more reps / same process
  circle the middle: *this is where things start to slip*
  "where's it breaking for you?"

The point isn't to look impressive.

It's to feel alive.

That's the part that matters.

Not the structure. Not the script.

Not even the angle of your camera or the size of the subtitles.

The authenticity. The absence of anything in you that needs it to work.

That's what makes people tune in.

CHAPTER 7:
PARETO PROSPECTING: TIME, TRIGGERS, MULTI-THREADING, AND DEMAND

Prospecting starts feeling unfair the second you realize it isn't a volume game.

It's a selection game with less fanfare than that UK show, *Take Me Out.*

And most reps aren't losing because they're lazy. They're losing because they're everywhere at once, which is the professional version of texting five people "what you doing tonight?" and still ending up alone with your phone, a DoorDash order, and the creeping sense that maybe *you're* the problem.

Effort is abundant. Precision is rare.

And the market rewards precision way more than it rewards effort, hustle, grinding, or whatever word people are using now to make disorganization sound noble.

That's where Pareto needs to stop being an idea to quote and start becoming a law. Not a cute little 80/20 graphic somebody posts with lock-in energy and no operating system behind it. *A law.* One you either obey, or end up with weeks that have "Spotify wrapped" energy for bad prospecting: 4,000 touches, seven actual signals, and your top genre was avoidance.

Roughly eighty percent of your results come from twenty percent of your inputs.

In dating, that means you get a tiny number of matches for every swipe. *Which is probably a good thing...*

In prospecting, it means a small fraction of your accounts, your hours, and your conversations are going to create nearly everything that becomes real pipeline. The rest is the business version of watching three seasons of a show in two days and calling it a recovery weekend.

The thing is, people understand Pareto intellectually and then build a workflow that completely disrespects it.

They say they're focused, then run an account list that looks like a Coachella lineup. Big. Ambitious. Totally unrealistic. Everybody's excited. Nobody's actually getting close enough to matter.

If your top ten accounts aren't getting at least half of your real thinking time, you don't have a strategy. You have shuffle mode.

Your calendar should look like a concentrated bet, not a diversified ETF of random activity. Your best hours should be reserved for the small set of accounts where something is actually in motion. Leadership changes. Missed numbers. Fundraising. A buying pattern is starting to stir under the polished exterior.

A lot of outbound looks like someone opened seventy-four browser tabs and called it market coverage. That's why prospecting has to become a spectrum, not a religion.

At the bottom of the org, speed matters more. Semi-automated outreach makes sense there because you're gathering signal, learning language, and figuring out what's actually happening versus what the company says is happening in a deck that definitely had six revisions, a designer, and one person fighting for the phrase "customer obsession."

Here, AI is useful.

If it helps you move faster without totally flattening your voice. If it acts like a sharp assistant, not like a machine that just drank three espressos and decided to rewrite the same sentence five hundred times in a tone called "confidently professional."

If it reads like slop, it gets treated like slop.

And everyone can tell. NPC dialogue. "Great insight." "Couldn't agree more." "This is the conversation we need to be having." "Please rescue my sheep, kind explorer."

The village remains cursed.

As you move up the account, everything slows down.

That's where a lot of reps get weird.

They keep using the same volume logic at executive levels and then act shocked when it dies. Sending a templated message to a VP is like sliding into a celebrity's DMs with "hey" and expecting a response. Technically possible. Socially awkward.

At higher levels, fewer touches matter more. More thought. More timing. More restraint. Because the higher you go, the more obvious it becomes when somebody is faking insight.

Repeating something from an earnings call isn't perspective.

It's subtitles.

Nobody's impressed by subtitles.

What cuts through is interpretation, aka *real insight.* Compressing what's happening into a point of view that feels like it came from inside the building, not from someone standing outside with a laptop trying to cosplay *Succession.*

You aren't trying to sound smart.

You're trying to sound right in a way that makes them pause.

That's where timing sharpens everything.

Most of the market chases loud triggers. Funding rounds. Press releases. Product launches. Big public moments everybody can see. Which means everybody is already there. The inbox is crowded, the angle is obvious, and you are the sixty-third person pretending the news created a reason to care.

The real trigger is usually hidden and way more actionable.

A job change not listed on their LinkedIn.

A new VP. A new CRO. A new CMO. Buried on page two in Google. Someone stepping into a role with blowtorch pressure they didn't create and expectations they can't avoid. They didn't inherit a clean slate. They inherited somebody else's mess and now need to move fast enough to look in control.

That's when everything compresses like a sixteen-car pileup, budgets break open, and vendors get pulled in.

People don't buy things because they've "reached enlightenment." They buy because they need momentum and can't afford to look passive.

FOMO is old. FOMU is worse: the fear of messing up.

Funding creates attention. Job changes create action. That's the trigger hierarchy.

If you track accounts, you see it late.

If you track people, you see it early.

And early is where the edge lives. Late is everybody posting the same take five minutes after it trends, and acting like they were the first person to describe the latest episode of *Euphoria* as "spicy".

There's a whole second category people miss, too.

Deadwood.

Closed-lost deals. Stalled evaluations. Threads everyone marked dead because they didn't close on the original timeline. Missed meeting reports. Old pricing requests or demo requests. They look dead. They're not dead.

Dead usually means early. Or mistimed. Or carried by the wrong person, or offered with too little impact.

One of the fastest ways to look smart in a new role isn't chasing a brand-new pipeline like a Labrador with a Slack notification. It's reopening what everyone else buried.

Run a won-deal analysis like you're Craig Elias, and patterns start showing up fast. Same titles. Same stakeholder cluster. Same internal title constellation over and over again.

Two VPs of IT. A CISO. A lead architect. A procurement blocker.

That's not a coincidence.

Once you see it, you know exactly how to multi-thread across active accounts and revive old deals. Now you're not just prospecting. You're reading shape.

That's how a line like this becomes powerful:

"Noticed you evaluated this six months ago."

That works because it respects reality and leads with contextual relevance.

You're not interrupting. You're re-entering. And re-entry beats interruption when the timing finally got honest.

There's also a difference between researching a company and actually experiencing it.

Most reps stay on the safe side of the glass.

Real signal lives on the other side.

You don't guess what their funnel feels like. You go through it.

Mystery shop them like *Undercover Boss* with a convincing goatee. Fill out the form. Call the number. Sit through the hold music like it's a cursed Spotify playlist from 2012.

Buy the product. Walk the store. Act like the customer. Read the brutal reviews. Then watch where the illusion breaks.

Something always breaks.

The response takes seventeen hours.

The messaging contradicts itself.

The SDR sounds like they're reading terms and conditions at gunpoint.

The follow-up dies after one touch like a situationship that swore it was just bad at texting.

That gap is an entry point.

"Went through your inbound flow, and your team took 17 hours to respond. Usually, that means either volume is off, or prioritization is."

Now you're not pitching. You're holding up a mirror.

People will argue with your opinion. They won't argue with their own funnel.

None of this matters, though, if there's no demand.

This is where most reps still lose the plot. They do the targeting, build the list, chase the trigger, maybe even get the timing right, and then send a message about upside.

Growth. Efficiency. Optimization. Potential.

Cool.

That's business catnip for people who enjoy nodding politely and doing absolutely nothing.

Every interaction is quietly answering one question:

"Why now?"

There are only a handful of reasons people act:

- Make money
- Protect money
- Reduce risk
- Meet a regulation
- Remove irritation

That's it. And they're not equal. Growth is attractive. Risk is urgent. Compliance is unavoidable. Irritation gets attention because it's already ruining somebody's day.

Upside gets filed. Pressure gets acted on.

Multi-threading is what makes all of this real.

No meaningful deal closes through one person. If you're relying on a single champion, a single director, a single thread, that's not strategy.

That's wishful thinking with a CRM. You work the account like a system. Bottom up for truth. Middle out for framing. Top down for urgency and budget.

Bottom-up tells you what's actually happening. Middle-out tells you how the problem is being translated across the org. Top-down tells you what consequences make action real.

That's groundswell. Intelligence moving up. The front lines give you insider signals you can quote to upper management when you warm call.

"Damn. You did your homework. I'm impressed."

And when it layers correctly, it becomes a beeswarm.

Not spam. Not chaos.

Coordinated awareness across the account. Crop circle Venns dropped like concert flyers on windshields. Multiple stakeholders are catching different angles of the same pressure until some rando CXO finally steps in and says the line you were waiting for:

"Hey, I'm the person handling this. Who made this and why do I kind of love it?"

That's the account revealing itself.

And this is where the tools matter, but only in the right order.

There's a split happening in sales right now, and it isn't between old school and modern. It's between people who can think in systems and people who still operate like human spreadsheets.

Technology Quotient (TQ) isn't about being *into AI* the way someone gets into cold plunges for six weeks and then makes it everyone's problem.

It's about seeing the board differently.

Enrichment layers.

Signal stacking.

Timing windows.

Sequencing logic.

All of it compresses time and sharpens judgment.

A rep using Clay or Claude well isn't just faster.

They're earlier. That's the edge. Earlier recognition.

But this isn't an AI prompt book, and it never will be.

Prompts are the new macros. Useful. Overrated. Rapidly commoditized.

Using AI without judgment is just outsourcing your personality to a very efficient intern.

That's why tool worship is such a dead end. The advantage isn't the software. The advantage is knowing what to look for, when to move, what not to automate, and what kind of thought actually deserves human fingerprints.

Because your real weapon is still older than any stack.

Acumen. Gravitas. Taste. Timing. The ability to think on your feet when the conversation stops being theoretical and starts getting expensive.

That's what separates the real operators from the empty suits with beautiful dashboards.

Most buyers say they don't want to talk to sales.

They also say they won't answer the phone.

And yet most real deals still close in actual conversations.

Amazing.

So everyone hates sales until they need a salesperson who can actually think.

Your greatest weapon isn't your workflow, your prompts, or the weekend you spent perfecting an automation like it's a side quest that somehow became your personality.

It's your ability to speak the language of leaders.

Outcomes. Risk. Tradeoffs. Pressure.

To read a P&L and understand how the business actually makes money instead of pitching features like it's demo day for a startup nobody funded.

Strategic prospecting is behavior change.

It's building consensus and pushing back. Staying in the awkward moment long enough for the truth to finally show up.

People buy the experience of being understood, not another perfectly structured message that sounds like it was assembled by a very confident robot.

If you use AI, use it to sharpen an assumptive point of view.

Not to write safer versions of things you were already too scared to say cleanly.

Your real software is courage.

Not downloadable. Not automated. No AI is taking that job.

You can spend twenty hours refining Claude workflows while another rep picks up the phone, has a few uncomfortable conversations, and stacks six figures in pipeline before lunch.

Use AI to remove twenty to forty percent of your admin.

Just don't confuse looking efficient with being effective.

Benioff hired thousands of human sellers to sell AI.

Riddle me that.

TAKEAWAY: HOW TO MAKE THE GAME FEEL UNFAIR

Stop prospecting like a cornball trying to answer every text in the group chat before somebody notices he has no actual plan.

Run the system.

Start with tiers. Tier 1 is active heat, live trigger, high-value accounts. Tier 2 is strong fit, but waiting on signal. Tier 3 is background noise until something changes.

Tier 1 gets your best hours. Not the weird half-conscious slot between an internal forecast call and lunch. Your best hours.

Then work triggers in the right order.

Funding gets attention. Job changes drive action. One gives you a generic excuse. The other drops you into urgency: a buyer who just inherited someone else's mess and needs to look competent before the quarter eats them alive.

Then reopen what everyone else buried. Closed-lost doesn't always mean wrong. It usually means early, mistimed, underpowered, or carried by the wrong person. Look at old deals and ask whether the pain disappeared or whether people just got tired.

Then send something that respects reality instead of pretending this is a fresh little romance.

"Noticed you looked at this six months ago. Guessing it either got less urgent or more expensive."

That works because it gives them something to react to, which is still much better than giving them nothing to feel.

Then, mystery shop.

Fill out the form. Call the number. Sit through the hold music from hell. Buy the thing if you can. Find the break. Use the break. Reference that unhinged review because where there's smoke, there's fire.

"Talked to your chatbot. Felt hollow. Submitted through your e-commerce form and waited two days for a callback."

Then multi-thread like an adult. Bottom-up for truth. Middle-out for framing. Top-down for consequence. Don't fall in love with one director and call it enterprise selling.

And use AI where it actually helps. Collecting research. Surfacing signals. Organizing accounts. Drafting options for Hyper-P.

Don't use it to fake conviction. Don't use it to manufacture taste. Don't use it to replace judgment. And definitely don't use it to write messages so polished they feel like they were approved by compliance and a nervous oat-milk latte.

That's how the game starts feeling unfair in all the best ways.

Not because you're *doing more.* Going fanatical 10X is how you speedrun burnout. The power law hands your sanity back before you can even finish saying Vilfredo Federico Damaso Pareto.

Because you finally stopped doing random acts of prospecting and started concentrating force where reality is already softening.

CHAPTER 8:

QUALIFICATION: IF THERE'S NO TENSION, THERE'S NO POINT

"We accept the love we think we deserve."

– Stephen Chbosky

In 2026, attention isn't just a currency. It's basically a relationship status, and most reps are stuck in a full-blown situationship with someone's indifference, like Drake waiting for Rihanna to unblock him in 2016, genuinely believing one more thoughtful follow-up is going to make the universe whisper back, "*seen and converted.*"

This is where modern selling became modern dating in a very obvious way, and nobody wants to admit it because the comparison feels a little too revealing.

Because what you're really doing when you over-explain a deal is the same thing somebody does when they triple-text "no pressure btw" at 1:47 a.m. You're auditioning for permanence in someone else's attention span. And attention span, in this era, is shorter than a TikTok apology video from a celebrity who absolutely read the comments before filming.

That's the first ugly truth.

Most deals don't die from rejection.

They die from comfort.

From being too safe, too available, too easy to delay. The same way nobody falls in love with the person who replies instantly, never misses a beat, and always says "happy to help!" like a customer support bot trained on LinkedIn optimism and herbal tea.

Because without tension, nothing has to happen.

And what doesn't have to happen *usually doesn't.*

Qualification isn't mainly about whether the account fits, whether the budget might exist, or whether somebody said your favorite little phrase, "this is definitely a priority for us," in a seductively hushed tone.

Qualification is about one thing:

Is there enough real tension here for this to move without you emotionally carrying it on your back like one of Jules' quirky little backpacks in *Euphoria*?

That's it.

After Pareto, you've already done the strategic part. You've picked better accounts. You've found the triggers. You've worked the signal. Now comes the harder part: deciding whether the thing in front of you actually deserves time, motion, and belief.

That's where most reps fail.

Because they're *romantics.*

They think activity is progress. They think responsiveness is momentum. They think a "good conversation" means anything. They think if the deal is still technically alive in the CRM, then something meaningful *must* still be happening beneath the surface.

Sometimes a deal isn't alive.

It's just warm. And warmth has tricked more reps than tequila and internal optimism combined.

No consequence, no decision.

No decision, no movement.

That's pipeline physics.

You see the same thing in elite sports before a trade deadline. Nobody moves when everybody's calm. Movement shows up when something becomes uncertain, when the Lakers suddenly might not want you anymore, when staying put starts to feel riskier than choosing. Decisions don't appear inside certainty. They appear when loss becomes visible.

That's what most qualification frameworks miss.

They make it sound like a checklist.

Need? Budget? Timeline? Authority?

Real qualification is asking a much sharper question:

"If nothing changes here, what happens?"

Because if the answer is "not much," then you don't have a live deal. You have curiosity, politeness, maybe even professional interest, but no tension.

And if there's no tension, there's no point.

If there's no cost to waiting, no cost to pausing, no cost to ignoring, then the system does what all systems do when inaction is free. It does *nothing.*

That's why some deals feel like a Netflix series nobody's actually bingeing. The algorithm keeps serving it up, you keep telling yourself it's "building toward something," and four episodes later, even the platform starts asking, "Are you still watching this or just emotionally attached to the idea of progress?"

A lot of pipeline is exactly that.

Once you see that, qualification stops being about keeping things alive and starts becoming about whether anything here deserves to continue.

That changes your behavior immediately. You stop trying to preserve the interaction and start testing it. You stop acting like the goal is to keep the vibe warm.

Because warm isn't enough, warm is how reps end up in emotional coworking arrangements with "maybe."

You know the type of deal. They reply. They're nice. They ask for something. They seem interested. They agree there's "definitely a challenge." They want to "keep talking." And yet somehow nothing materializes. Nobody owns the pain. No one can tell you *why now*. No one can explain what happens if this slips another quarter. There's no real consequence, just ambient concern in a nice blazer.

And the reason reps stay inside those deals too long is simple: qualifying honestly is more emotionally demanding than nurturing a fantasy. Fantasy lets you stay hopeful. Qualification forces you to ask whether the thing has bones.

For reps to achieve anything in this world, they need to be "pickier". They need to separate:

- Real urgency from polite interest
- Momentum from maintenance
- Conversation from consequence
- A live deal from an emotionally sponsored hobby

Because once you're treating everything the same way, you're performing CPR on maybe one real opportunity amongst a sea of plastic dummies.

And you're giving them all the same energy, even when *only one* has a chance of responding. That's desperation. It's preservation at its worst.

Because once you're preserving, consequence disappears.

The other side has no reason to move. They can stay in the interaction forever, consuming your attention like it's a streaming subscription they forgot to cancel.

In dating, this shows up even faster. The person who's always available becomes the person who never gets chased. There's no cost to delay, no cost to pause, no cost to ignore.

Meanwhile, the person who doesn't overextend becomes psychologically louder. Their silence isn't empty. It's loaded. It suggests that continuation isn't guaranteed, and that's where curiosity turns into attention.

Think about how celebrity dynamics actually work. When Taylor Swift disappears from the public eye for a moment, the internet doesn't relax. It escalates. When Travis Kelce is suddenly less visible, the narrative intensifies. Nobody leans in when everything is constantly available. They lean in when access becomes uncertain.

Sales works the same way, even if everyone pretends it doesn't.

The SDR who responds instantly to everything thinks they are being "responsive." But what they are actually doing is flattening the entire emotional graph of the interaction. No highs, no lows, no tension, no reason to move. Just a calm, endless plateau of polite irrelevance.

And the founder who never creates space thinks speed equals leverage. But speed without contrast is just white noise at a higher frequency.

What actually creates movement is the interruption of certainty.

Because now there's something to lose.

This is why the best operators don't behave like pursuers.

They behave like filters.

Like Timothée Chalamet and Kylie Jenner. Or Justin and Hailey Bieber. Nobody's chasing. They're both the pick.

They're not trying to keep every conversation alive. They're allowing conversations to either justify continuation or dissolve cleanly. No becoming the emotional WiFi extender for a signal that was never really transmitting anything.

That's what qualification looks like at a high level.

Not pressure. Not aggression. Just truth with enough backbone to survive silence.

That truth usually comes from the questions you ask. Not vague discovery questions designed to make the room feel collaborative. Real diagnostic questions. Questions that introduce cost to inertia. Questions that make the deal tell on itself.

Poke the wound and twist the knife.

"What happens if nothing changes from here?"

That one matters because it removes the luxury of pretending motion equals progress. Suddenly, inaction has a shape. It stops being neutral.

"Why now?"

That one hits harder. If it's real, it's instant. No slow burn. Your body knows before your brain catches up. Switch flips. Hair up. Static in the air. *Big deal energy.*

If it doesn't hit, no amount of polishing, enthusiasm, or tasteful follow-up copy is going to create it for them. Silence becomes clarity wearing no makeup.

"What actually makes this worth solving for you?"

That removes you from the center of the story entirely. It stops being about your value, your effort, your framing, your timing. It becomes about whether they have enough internal gravity to pull this forward without you acting like the *little engine that could.*

That's where most reps fold.

Because folding feels like control compared to silence.

So they jump in. Clarify. Soften. Rescue. They become the emotional support animal for an opportunity that still hasn't demonstrated a pulse. They keep talking because action feels better than admitting that maybe this thing was never really moving at all.

But nothing real ever moves because one person is doing all the believing.

At that point, you're not in a conversation anymore.

You're a one-man documentary maker, narrating a second participant who never agreed to be filmed.

That's the hidden cost. Not rejection.

Time spent inside "almosts" that behave like progress but function like loops.

If there is mutual pull, it moves.

If there isn't, it dissolves without drama.

That's qualification.

Not BANT with a skincare routine.

Not fake curiosity in a Notion template.

Not "strong relationship" energy because they replied to your email in under 48 hours.

Qualification is the discipline of refusing to confuse politeness with motion, responsiveness with consequence, and interest with cost.

Without tension, there's no reason to decide.

Without a reason to decide, there's no reason to move.

And if there's no movement, you don't have a deal.

You have a beautifully maintained *maybe.*

TAKEAWAY: HOW TO STOP BABYSITTING DEAD DEALS

On your next ten active opportunities, stop asking:

"How do I keep this warm?"

That's not qualification. That's babysitting.

Ask better questions:

- What happens if they do nothing?
- Why now?
- Who actually feels this?
- What slips if this waits another quarter?
- Am I carrying the whole interaction?

Fake momentum has tells. They're responsive, but vague. They want more info, but can't define urgency. They agree the problem exists, but can't name the cost. They like the conversation, but only while you supply all the energy, structure, and next steps.

That's not a live deal. That's a podcast. And if you keep calling it "momentum," you're not qualifying, you're gaslighting yourself with calendar invites.

So stop asking questions that revolve around trying to keep the interaction alive. Ask questions that expose whether it actually *deserves* to live.

Then watch your own behavior.

If you're re-explaining the same point, you're probably preserving. If you're replying instantly to maintain warmth, you're probably preserving. If the deal only feels alive while you're in the room, you're definitely preserving. If you're supplying urgency they never supply themselves; it isn't real.

You're not there to keep every deal breathing. You're there to find out which deals actually have lungs.

And yes, this is the part where a lot of reps get uncomfortable, because letting a deal reveal itself feels riskier than constantly "adding value."

But most of what gets called value is really just maintenance in nicer language. If you're trying to preserve every deal like it's *Love Island,* and if you don't stay moderately interesting, you'll get "voted off," you're missing the point.

Don't do hospice in HubSpot.

Do the diagnosis.

Because when you stop confusing motion with momentum, something useful happens. You get your time back. You get your standards back. You get your leverage back.

And the deals that remain start behaving very differently. They gain momentum. They ask better questions. They move without being emotionally supervised. You're pursuing a relationship that can actually survive, rather than wasting all your time on Tinder matches who say they "might" be up for a meeting at "some point."

Qualification isn't about making more things survive.

It's about making sure only the real things do.

CHAPTER 9:

FOLLOW-UPS, RE-ENTRY & CATCH AND RELEASE: CHASE TOO MUCH AND IT'S ALREADY DONE

"The less one thinks of oneself, the more powerful one becomes."

– Fyodor Dostoevsky

Follow-ups are where the pipeline goes to get weird.

Nothing's dead, nothing's alive, and everything's stuck in that cursed modern in-between where both sides are still technically connected, but nobody's actually choosing anything anymore. It's a *Love Is Blind* season where everybody keeps saying, "I just need a little more time to process," and somehow nobody ever gets to the altar.

That's most B2B pipeline.

It's the sales version of being left on delivered by someone who still watches your stories. Present, aware, vaguely engaged, absolutely not deciding. The same energy as NBA trade rumors that generate sixteen podcasts, forty-three tweets, and one fake Woj graphic from an account called something like @RealHoopsInsiderrr, only for nothing to happen and everyone to act like the emotional chaos counted as a transaction.

And in business, we call this *professionalism.*

Just following up. Just circling back. Just checking in.

It sounds procedural. Responsible. Mature. Like one of those phrases people type while nodding at themselves in a Google Doc. But underneath, it's the corporate version of texting "hey you" to someone who already demoted you from possibility to background presence but hasn't formally closed the tab because closure requires energy nobody has.

Most follow-ups don't fail because they're rude, clumsy, or wildly mistimed. They fail because they come back without changing the emotional weather. No new signal. No new frame. No new tension. No reason for the nervous system on the other side to treat this like anything other than a sequel it didn't ask for.

The first message can still feel like intrigue. The second might still land as tolerance. By the third, if nothing fundamental has shifted, you've just become the iOS update they keep postponing: visible, mildly annoying, and somehow never urgent enough to deal with.

That's why follow-ups fail. Not because they're wrong. Because they're familiar.

Familiarity turns you from "potential opportunity" into "something I'll deal with later," which is the same psychological category as unread emails, unopened tabs, and every app you swore you'd delete two phones ago but now just live around.

That's why "just checking in" isn't harmless. It's revealing. It confirms that nothing's changed, nothing's evolved, and the conversation's still alive only on your side of the system.

That gap is where deals gradually die while everyone still behaves professionally in Slack threads and forecast meetings and those deeply fake "good momentum here" recaps.

Most pipelines don't collapse from some dramatic "no." They collapse from a *sameness overdose*. Saturation. Too many touches without transformation turn you from signal into environment. You stop being something they engage with and become something they exist around. Like traffic. Like ads. Like that one coworker who always says, "quick question" and never once, in the history of language, means *quick*.

That's why pipelines turn into situationships.

Because both sides are still technically in it, but nobody's actually moving anything forward. It's just messages floating through time, each one slightly more redundant than the last, like two people saying "we should catch up soon" until the phrase loses all semantic meaning and becomes a ceremonial lie.

Underneath all of this is a truth people hate because it ruins effort-based identity:

The brain doesn't reward effort.

It rewards change.

That means every follow-up without evolution doesn't increase your chance of response. It deepens your predictability inside their system. And once predictability sets in, attention doesn't fight you. It simply stops needing you.

That's the beginning of the end.

The internet broke people a little here. It trained everyone to believe consistency is always good. Post every day. Follow up every few days. Stay top of mind. Show up. Be visible. Keep going.

That works if you're a fitness creator filming discipline content in front of a white wall and a ring light. It doesn't work if the person on the other side of your message is already filtering ninety percent of the world on instinct, and all you've done is become another item on their internal furniture list.

Consistency without variation isn't presence.

It's wallpaper.

And nobody really *lusts* after wallpaper.

RE-ENTRY, NOT CONTINUATION

The fix isn't "follow up better."

It's to stop trying to revive the dead thing.

High performers don't win because they follow up more. They win because they reappear differently. They disappear long enough for emotional residue to decay, then they come back like a new moment entered the system. No apology arc. No "just checking in." No weird little continuity debt hanging off the message like a tote bag full of your previous disappointment.

Just clean re-entry into a new frame.

"You're probably still dealing with this. Worth revisiting?"

That works because the past no longer has jurisdiction over the present moment. The brain's no longer processing repetition. It's processing novelty with context.

This is where most people get confused. They think the second message should somehow build on the first one, like the first note accumulated emotional equity, and now the sequel should honor the canon. It didn't. The prospect isn't sitting there replaying your outreach like it's a Taylor Swift bridge with hidden clues and emotional debt.

The first message either opened something or it didn't. If it didn't, dragging it forward only strengthens the category. If it did, your next move still can't arrive as a stale continuation. It has to feel like the moment changed shape.

That's re-entry.

Not "following up on my last note." Not "wanted to bring this back to the top of your inbox." Not "hope this didn't slip through."

Those are all just different versions of saying, "The last attempt didn't work, so I'm now asking you to acknowledge the failure with a polite response."

No thanks.

You don't say "following up" because the phrase itself smells like burden. It tells the brain exactly what this is: an obligation being re-presented in a slightly different suit.

Instead, you enter like the frame reset itself.

"Feels like this either matters now or it doesn't."

"You're probably still dealing with this."

"Still a priority?"

"What's the good word?"

That's different. It doesn't sound like a reminder. It sounds like a new decision.

And that's the real game.

Attention isn't linear. It's reset-based.

Songs resurface years later. Athletes disappear for a season and then suddenly own the timeline in one playoff run. Public figures vanish, say nothing, then re-enter with one perfect moment, and the internet acts like they never left. Nobody experiences those returns as *continued effort*. They experience them as a reset in relevance.

Same thing here.

Every follow-up either resets the frame or confirms you're still trapped inside the last one.

That's it.

And yes, this is where sales and flirting fully collapse into the same operating system.

The brain has already decided what you are before it finishes reading you. Not consciously, but like Netflix autoplay. It sees "follow-up," recognizes the genre, and swipes left without drama.

No rejection. No confrontation. Just emotional buffering and then nothing.

People think persistence is the problem. It isn't. The real issue is timing dressed up as effort. It's Ross from *Friends* showing up with a PowerPoint explaining why the relationship deserves another shot after the room already moved on emotionally three episodes ago.

The shift is in how you re-enter.

No memory. No residue. No trying to revive a dead scene like it accidentally got cut from the final edit and now deserves director's commentary. You arrive like the emotional weather changed while nobody was looking.

Attention is never deserved.

It's triggered.

And triggers don't come from explanation.

They come from disruption.

That's why the best second message often doesn't feel like a second message at all. It feels like déjà vu with a different outcome. A fresh scene with old familiarity embedded inside it.

You don't follow up.

You re-enter the frame like nothing closed.

A reminder asks them not to forget.

A re-entry gives them a reason not to want to.

That's a huge difference.

FLIRTING IS PROSPECTING

Flirting is prospecting.

Prospecting is flirting.

Both are about timing, not effort. Both are about implication, not over-explanation. Both kill the vibe the second one side starts trying to secure the outcome instead of letting the moment breathe.

Nobody wants to say that because it sounds unserious and a little dangerous, but it's true.

Think about the difference between seduction and negotiation.

One invites.

The other explains.

One lets the other person lean forward. The other keeps filing paperwork about why the interaction should continue.

That's exactly what happens in follow-up sequences.

Bad reps negotiate. They explain. They restate. They provide more context. They turn every lull into a mini TED Talk about why they still deserve attention. In dating, that turns you from a serious "option" into a meme someone shares on the r/NiceGuys subreddit. In sales, it turns you into someone people actively go out of their way to ignore.

Good reps imply. They shift the signal. They re-enter with just enough pressure removed, and just enough novelty added that the other person has to step in voluntarily.

That's why Ryan Gosling works so well in *Crazy, Stupid, Love* with Emma Stone. The power's not in him dumping information. It's in the restraint between the lines. He doesn't chase resolution. He creates tension, she meets it, and they let it hang just long enough for curiosity to do the work.

Same thing in *Euphoria*, especially with Jules Vaughn. The tension between characters works because nothing resolves cleanly. Every text, every glance, every pause carries unfinished emotional data. The second someone forces clarity too early, the entire dynamic dies into boredom. The same thing happens in sales, but nobody calls it trauma; they call it "pipeline hygiene."

And that's why most follow-ups fail.

They explain when they should imply. They negotiate when they should reset. They show up like they're defending their right to exist in someone's attention span.

That lowers you instantly.

The moment the other person feels you need the reply more than they need the answer, the frame flips. You become the one waiting. And the second you're waiting, you're no longer interesting.

That's a brutal rule, but it's useful.

Love Island is basically a lab experiment in re-entry. Nobody wins by continuing the same energy forever. They disappear, recouple, betray, go quiet, reappear, and the people who keep attention are never the loudest. They're the ones who understand when a dynamic is dead, when it's dormant, and when to step back in with changed energy.

That's all re-entry is.

Reappearing at the exact emotional inflection point where the moment hasn't died, it just went quiet.

The right move isn't to rebuild the moment.

It's to reactivate it.

That requires less narration, less continuity debt, less emotional insistence, and more trust in the fact that if the energy's still there, a cleaner signal will bring it back.

Flirting isn't a pursuit. It's a calibrated return.

That's also what great prospecting looks like after the first touch.

CATCH AND RELEASE: REMOVE PRESSURE AND WATCH WHAT RETURNS

"The less you reveal, the more people can wonder."

– Emma Watson

Once you understand re-entry, the next mistake becomes obvious.

You reconnect cleanly and then immediately suffocate the interaction again.

The modern attention economy isn't really a marketplace anymore. It's a group chat where everybody's typing, nobody's relaxed, and the moment you look like you need a reply, you get silently muted like a bad Drake remix.

That's the psychological operating system underneath modern persuasion, whether you call it sales, dating, or just trying not to get left on delivered by someone who's definitely online, chatting to someone else.

Most people still live under the illusion that more effort creates more connection. More clarity. More context. More reassurance. More "just wanted to make sure this didn't get lost." But the brain doesn't reward completion.

It rewards tension.

The second something feels emotionally secure, over-explained, or too eager to continue itself, it gets categorized and dropped like a Netflix show you already understand the ending of. This is why the real leverage point isn't the message.

It's the absence of need behind the message.

The moment your energy signals "I need this to land," the interaction changes tone, the way a Marvel villain walks on screen, and starts monologuing way too soon. The audience feels the problem before they understand it. They don't consciously reject it. They drift.

Same way you drift past an influencer explaining discipline while clearly avoiding the gym with Olympic creativity.

What actually moves people isn't continuity.

It's re-entry followed by release.

You make contact, and then you refuse to trap the interaction. You don't over-secure it. You don't force the emotional arc to keep running. You remove enough pressure that the other person can either lean back in or finally show you there was nothing there to begin with.

That's real control.

Not ghosting. Not games. Not "playing hard to get" like a guy who just discovered scarcity on LinkedIn and now thinks silence is a strategy.

Pressure removal.

A lot of people hear "leave space" and immediately start cosplaying aloofness. The move isn't a disappearance. It isn't punishment. It isn't fake indifference. It isn't trying to become mysterious through emotional smoke machines.

It's simply refusing to carry both halves of the exchange.

That's very different.

Most reps unknowingly become over-invested side characters in their own outreach, constantly trying to secure emotional continuity. The other side feels the weight.

And weight kills curiosity.

You can see it everywhere once you notice it. The friend who replies instantly to every single thing eventually becomes background texture. The brand that always pushes becomes invisible. The person who never leaves space becomes predictable and then irrelevant.

Even in celebrity culture, the same rule applies. Rihanna disappears slightly, and the internet gets louder about her. Messi says almost nothing off the field and somehow feels more present than half the people posting twelve times a day. Overexposure doesn't create pull.

It turns people into content.

Presence without need is different.

That's what catch and release creates.

Human attention is structured around unfinished loops. The brain hates unresolved patterns more than it hates silence. That's why cliffhangers outperform conclusions. It's why a line that hangs slightly open stays alive longer than a polished paragraph that answers every possible question like it was reviewed by Legal, HR, and Trevor from Accounts Payable in Omaha, who always says, "Let's take this offline."

This is also where people misread distance. They think distance means disinterest, so they increase effort. Effort increases pressure. Pressure increases distance. Distance confirms their fear. And then they tell themselves the lead went cold.

Maybe.

Or maybe you hugged the life out of it.

The shift's simple and ruthless. Stop trying to complete the interaction on your side. Stop trying to solve silence like it's a technical bug. Let the exchange hang slightly open and then watch what returns.

Because what returns is what still has energy.

Not what you forced. Not what you explained. Not what you chased like a subplot in a reality show that got canceled before the reunion episode.

You stop following up to maintain vague warmth. You stop trying to finish the emotional exchange for both people. You let space do what space does: expose reality.

That makes you calmer. Cleaner. Harder to classify. Less easy to ignore. And weirdly, yes, slightly more attractive in every room where attention matters.

Because you stopped being trapped inside your own need for continuation.

Release isn't surrender.

It's not "whatever, never mind." It's not pouting in a nicer font. It's not passive aggression pretending to be detachment. It's not disappearing and hoping mystery does your job for you. Release is pressure removal plus observation.

You remove the chokehold, then you watch the truth unfold.

A few lines that do this cleanly:

- "Happy to drop this if it's not relevant."
- "Might not be a priority right now."
- "If this isn't a Q3 priority, no stress."
- "Not sure this is live enough to keep poking at."
- "Feels like this either matters or it doesn't, both fine."

Those lines work because they stop negotiating with silence. They relieve the other person of the obligation to keep pretending. And the second obligation leaves, one of two things happens:

They step in.

Or they don't.

That's the result you needed all along.

BOOKED TO HELD: DON'T LET THE MEETING DIE IN THE CALENDAR

A booked meeting is just another place where reps accidentally become awkward.

A 70% show rate means three out of ten meetings disappear. That's not "just how it is." That's a leak. The reps who fix this are often at 90%+, and the difference isn't more reminders.

It's how they manage the emotional space between booked and held.

People don't no-show because calendars broke.

They no-show for the same reason dates ghost after saying, "this was fun."

The moment expired.

You weren't relevant enough. You weren't compelling enough. You didn't hit anything that actually mattered.

No pain, no sale. No pain, no show.

By the time the meeting hits, you're competing with inbox chaos, internal politics, and the god-tier seduction of "I'll just deal with this later." You didn't lose the meeting because calendars are chaotic. You lost it because the energy expired, and nothing in the chasm made showing up feel more relevant than postponing thought altogether.

Trying to fix that with needy reminders is where it gets tragic. Long confirmations. Double pings. "Just checking, haha." It's the corporate version of texting "you up?" twice and pretending the second time was somehow more casual.

Needy is creepy.

The move is to hold the line between presence and pressure. Persistent, patient, never desperate. You stay in it without grabbing at it.

That means the day before message isn't a reminder.

It's a re-hook.

Quick text or short email:

"Quick prep for tomorrow, anything you want to make sure we cover?"

Morning-of stays clean:

"On for 10?"

Anchored beats abstract every time.

And if you want to elevate it, add one line of tension before the call or the meeting. Not a pitch. Just a hook.

"Quick thought before we jump on, most teams realize mid-call they've been solving the wrong problem."

Now it's not just a meeting.

It's a moment.

People skip meetings all the time. They don't skip moments that might actually shift something.

But none of this saves you if the first interaction was mid. If you didn't surface real pain, or better, latent pain, the meeting was optional from the start. You didn't create tension.

You created a calendar event.

And calendar events get ghosted all the time. Worse, they often get lost in spam folders thanks to the help of an overly protective email filter. That's why I tend to stay on the call until the invite gets accepted. No way they can give me the "I never saw the invite" line then.

This whole thing is finesse. Like speed dating or longboarding, staying a little too long kills it. Too much pressure and the thing collapses. Too little presence and it fades. The reps who understand this don't chase the meeting.

They keep the moment alive just enough that showing up feels natural.

Because in the end, this isn't about reminders.

It's about not becoming easy to forget.

TAKEAWAY: HOW TO STOP FOLLOWING UP LIKE A BURDEN

On your next ten active opportunities, stop thinking in terms of "how do I keep this warm?"

That's not a strategy. That's emotional crockpot behavior.

Think in terms of stages instead.

Is this stale continuity?

Does this need re-entry?

Am I re-entering cleanly?

Am I overholding the moment after I reconnect?

If a meeting is booked, am I keeping it alive or making it weird?

That's the operating system. From there, stop continuing "dead energy".

Don't send:

- Just checking in
- Circling back
- Following up on my last note
- Wanted to see if you had any thoughts
- Just wanted to make sure this didn't get lost

Those lines don't revive anything. They confirm you're still emotionally living in the old thread.

If nothing's changed in their world, in your point of view, or in the emotional temperature of the thread, you probably don't have a re-entry.

You've got a reminder pulling the morning-after exit, hoodie up, avoiding eye contact.

Good re-entry lines:

- "You're probably still dealing with this. Worth revisiting?"
- "Feels like this either matters now or it doesn't, both fine."
- "Could be bad timing. No issue if so."
- "Might not be a priority right now. Should I close it out?"
- "Not sure this is live enough to keep poking at."

These works because they feel current, not burdened.

And once the new frame lands, don't immediately smother it with context. Don't take a clean signal and turn it into a TED Talk. If you send, "This may be irrelevant or useful, not sure which yet," don't follow it with a paragraph about transformational outcomes across multiple verticals. Let the pause do its job.

Good release lines:

- "Happy to drop this if it's not relevant."
- "Might not be a priority right now."
- "No issue if the timing's off."
- "Feels like this may not be live enough to keep chasing."

That's not weakness.

That's pressure removal. And pressure removal often creates the relief that brings the room back to life.

Finally, keep booked meetings alive. Stay on the call until they accept, then jump in just before the big moment. The day-before note isn't a reminder; it's a re-hook. For a 100% show rate, stay on the line while they find the invite and accept it in real time.

This is your power close as an SDR: when the silence hits, embrace it. Most reps can't handle those few seconds, but your calm tone and composure are what win the meeting.

Try:

- "Quick prep for tomorrow, anything you want to make sure we cover?"
- "Still good for 2 tomorrow? Anything you want us locked in for?"

Morning of:

- "On for 10?"
- "Still good for 3 at the lobby café?"
- "See you after your 9:30?"

And if you want more pull:

"Quick thought before we jump on, most teams realize pretty fast they've been solving the wrong layer of the problem."

That's enough.

If your meeting-confirmation note sounds like a paragraph trying to emotionally secure attendance, cut it in half, then cut it in half again.

When you stop carrying the interaction, one of two things happens.

It returns.

Or it doesn't.

If it returns, it usually comes back with more ownership, less vagueness, and more gravity. If it doesn't, then good. You learned the truth before wasting six more weeks pretending the pipeline was just early.

That's how you stop following up like a burden and start reappearing like a decision.

CHAPTER 10:

TIMING AND ESCALATION

"Gather the rosebuds while you may."

– Robert Herrick

There's a version of timing most people think they understand until they've missed enough live moments to realize they absolutely don't. They call it patience, discipline, or emotional control. What they're actually doing is stepping half an inch outside the moment, folding their arms, and calling it wisdom, like someone watching a party through tinted glass and insisting they're still somehow on the dance floor.

That's what makes timing such a brutal thing to teach. It almost never fails in obvious ways. Nobody gets a push notification from the universe saying, "Hey, just a heads-up, that opportunity you were carefully emotionally calibrating? Gone now."

It fails invisibly. Cleanly. Politely. A room that was warm goes neutral. A prospect who was leaning in goes informational. A date that had chemistry becomes two people discussing podcasts with the dead sincerity of a regional airport wine bar.

And the whole thing usually starts the same way: You get careful. Then you get awkward.

Not cartoon awkward. Not guy-spills-water-on-himself-and-blames-Mercury-retrograde awkward. More dangerous than that. The kind of careful awkwardness that looks mature if you've never actually closed anything difficult. You slow your response just enough to feel composed. You add just enough extra context so nothing can be misunderstood. You start optimizing your words the way Meta optimizes ads: heavily tested, technically improved, spiritually dead.

And in that exact moment, you're no longer in the moment.

You're managing it.

Which sounds responsible until you realize nobody has ever been seduced, recruited, promoted, closed, or chosen because someone "managed the interaction beautifully." That's not how momentum works. That's how airport staff explain why your gate changed, and your will to live should too.

The truth is, moments don't wait for clarity. They behave more like NBA fast breaks than boardroom strategies. If the lane opens and you hesitate, the lane closes. Nobody stops the game, so you can admire how emotionally intelligent you're being about it. The defender recovers. The opening's gone. And then you get to spend the next five minutes pretending the worst option was actually more strategic.

That's the hidden cruelty in timing.

The window closes politely.

Real life gets a vote again. Optionality walks back into the room. The heat goes out.

And it almost always begins with the same internal lie:

"I should be thoughtful here."

No.

You should be *present* here.

Thoughtfulness is what your brain reaches for when it wants to exit the moment without admitting it's scared of misalignment. Presence is riskier because presence means responding at the speed of truth, not at the speed of self-protection. Truth doesn't usually need a committee. It doesn't open a side tab, draft four versions, and pick the safest one. Truth says the next necessary thing and lets reality deal with its own emotions.

That's why so many otherwise smart people keep almost converting moments for years. They're losing because they feel the shift and then try to become impressive instead of aligned. They step back into their heads and start narrating themselves like they're starring in a tasteful A24 film called *Man Who Nearly Sent The Right Email.*

A lot of hesitation gets rebranded as maturity because that sounds less humiliating.

Usually, it's just fear with a decent haircut.

Once you know what to look for, you see this everywhere.

A prospect starts in browse mode. Their questions are broad, clean, noncommittal.

"What exactly do you do?"

"How are teams using this?"

"How are you different from what we already have?"

Fine.

That's still the lobby.

Don't act like you've been invited into the penthouse because somebody asked where the elevator is.

Then something changes.

The tone settles. The questions get pointed. They stop asking about your thing in the abstract and start asking about their world in the concrete.

"How would this work in our environment?"

"How long would this take to stand up?"

"Who usually owns this internally?"

"What does rollout look like if we tested it in one region?"

"Would this sit with ops or with leadership?"

That's not curiosity.

That's a transition.

That's the room moving from interest into consequence. They're trying you on mentally. They're locating friction, politics, timing, ownership, risk, effort, and blowback. They're not flirting with the concept anymore. They're asking whether this thing could survive in their ecosystem without setting off alarms.

That shift is everything. *And it's fragile.*

This is where average reps become the spiritual equivalent of a man whipping out a slideshow right at the moment the house party gets interesting, and someone suggests Jello shots. They think they need to be more complete, more helpful, more structured, more consultative, which usually means they start answering like a premium FAQ page.

And that's how they kill momentum.

They step in late.

Timing is the real currency in conversion. Not persuasion. Not logic. Not value delivery. *Timing.* Because timing is what tells reality whether something's still alive or whether it has already started becoming memory.

Same thing happens in dating, which means this chapter is also about your personality, whether you like it or not. A pause lasts just a little too long. Eye contact doesn't bounce away immediately. A question carries subtext instead of politeness. The room changes.

Chemistry shows up in a tiny skirt and starts making people stammer.

Then one person, almost always the more frightened one, tries to make the moment safer. They add more language. More comfort. More explanation. They turn something alive into something manageable.

And the chemistry leaves like it got a better offer.

That's the tragedy.

Most people don't miss live moments because they lack charm. They miss them because they tried to protect the moment instead of continuing it.

Protection is where heat goes to die.

That's also why high performers often look fast even when they're not naturally aggressive people. They're not moving faster because they're pushy. They're moving faster because they're synchronized. They're not guessing. They're not forcing. They're matching. They hear the beat and don't miss it.

A weak rep thinks, "How do I advance this?"

A strong rep thinks, "What is this already becoming?"

That second question is where timing lives.

ESCALATION ISN'T FORCE. IT'S CONTINUATION.

Most people hear the word escalation and immediately picture force.

Too much energy. Too much urgency. Too much "let's get something on the calendar." Too much podcast-thumbnail confidence from a man in a quarter-zip who says "book more meetings" like it's both a philosophy and a skin-care routine.

That's *lunging*.

Real escalation doesn't feel like escalation from the inside. It feels like continuity. Like the next beat in a song that was already playing. Nobody at a Travis Scott concert thinks, "Interesting, the beat has now escalated." They just move. That's how great next steps work. They don't feel imported. They feel discovered.

Escalation is saying the next necessary thing while the room can still carry it.

Once you get that, the whole thing gets cleaner.

If a prospect shifts from "what do you do?" to "how would this work in our environment?" then the next necessary thing might be pressure-testing it live, bringing the right people into the room, giving ownership shape, or moving from concept to specifics.

What it almost never is, is another three-minute explainer, a recap of your differentiators, seven extra examples no one asked for, or a timid little "would you maybe potentially be open to…" line that sounds like your self-esteem is outsourcing its decision-making.

Good escalation has spine.

But it doesn't feel heavy.

It's direct without feeling abrupt. It names the obvious next move without making the room feel handled by a man who once described himself as a "full-stack closer" and meant it.

So instead of:

"Totally, and just to give you more context around how we partner with teams like yours…"

You get:

"Feels like we've moved past theory here."

Instead of:

"I'd be happy to send over some more information if that's helpful."

You get:

"This sounds worth looking at properly."

Instead of:

"Would you be open to maybe continuing the conversation if it makes sense on your side?"

You get:

"If this is real on your side, we should probably stop talking around it."

Or:

"Easier to walk through than explain. Tomorrow at two or Thursday morning?"

That's escalation done right. Not because it's aggressive. Because the room already earned it.

The two ways people blow this are very predictable.

They go too early.

Or they go too late.

Going too early is easier to spot because it feels like panic in more expensive cosmetics. The prospect says, "Yeah, that's been a challenge," and the rep starts acting like procurement should already be crying. Suddenly, they want to bring in legal, security, finance, and perhaps a priest.

Relax. This isn't *The Bachelor*.

No one's proposing mid-appetizer.

That's over-escalation. It happens when somebody hears one promising answer and mistakes movement for commitment.

Going too late is subtler and more common. The room changes, the prospect leans in, the next move becomes obvious, and the rep gets thoughtful. They answer too much. They explain too much. They keep teaching because teaching feels safer than asking for motion. By the time they finally suggest the next step, the moment that would've carried it is gone, and now the ask feels like admin.

That's how people turn chemistry into onboarding.

The sweet spot is narrower than people want it to be. Escalation should feel like the next beat, not a jump cut. The next obvious thing, not the next impressive thing.

That's why elite performers in every field talk so much about feel. Kobe didn't need a committee meeting before taking the shot. He felt the defender shift and acted before language caught up. Comedy works the same way. Say the punchline too late, and you don't exactly bomb; you just become irrelevant mid-sentence. George Clooney doesn't wait for perfect social calibration in a scene. He lands the line when tension peaks, not after it's been explained to death by a nervous internal producer.

In influence, irrelevance is worse than rejection.

Rejection at least admits you were in the room.

Irrelevance means you arrived after the room had already moved on and then tried to recreate the heat using rational inputs, which is basically trying to relight a flame with spreadsheets and thought leadership.

That never works.

THE OUTBOUND DAILY OPERATING LOOP

Timing isn't just instinct.

It's exposure.

People who catch live moments consistently aren't usually blessed by the gods of charisma. They're in enough motion, often enough, that they recognize the shift when it appears. They've built a system that gives them real reps, real signals, real live contact, and enough pattern recognition to know when a room has turned.

That's what the operating loop is for.

Not to turn you into a robot.

To put you in enough live situations that timing stops feeling mystical and starts feeling normal.

Winning in outbound is still a consistency game. It's still a marathon. But not in that corny "just trust the process" way people say right before spending six hours reorganizing Salesforce fields instead of talking to a human being. It's a marathon because repetition builds feel. And feel is what lets you recognize transition, move cleanly, and stop arriving late to your own opportunities.

Start by building fresh surface area every day.

Add 20 to 40 new executives a day. That's 400 to 800 a month. Blank connect. Don't write a tiny admissions essay in the request. Don't soft-launch your personality. Just connect.

Then message everyone who adds you back:

"what's your big vision for 202X?"

It's simple, open, and easy to answer without triggering the internal seller alarm.

Use your InMails too. All of them. Don't save them like wartime rations. Around 20 a day if you've got them. Hoarding outreach inventory is how people stay strategic and quietly irrelevant.

The point of this first layer isn't brilliance.

It's surface area.

You can't catch moments you never create contact for.

Then work live signals, not just static lists. Three times a day, check profile views, likes, comments, connection accepts, and any little micro-engagement that suggests somebody noticed you. Then act on them. Call those people. DM those people. Use the heat while it's *still hot.*

Work TeamLink too. Warm intros from colleagues. Warm referrals. Ghostwrite the intro when needed, because "happy to connect you two" is often executive code for "please do all of this for me so I can feel helpful with zero labor."

Then create direct contact every day. Send 5 to 10 tailored voice or video drops. Not because video is magic, but because tone carries more trust than polished text ever will. Run 30 outbound touch sequences a day. Triple if there's no sequencer running: call, voicemail, email. Double if an email sequencer is already running: call and voicemail. Don't pile sloppy overlap on top of machine overlap and call it omnichannel.

That's how you become spam in surround sound.

Keep the whole VM touch under 90 seconds if possible. Tight. Sharp. Done.

Nobody needs your NPR interview.

Leave 4 to 5 hyper-personalized voicemails over time per prospect. Not because one voicemail changes destiny. Because repetition with variation creates familiarity without flattening into sameness. Max profile scan: 30 seconds. This isn't *Dateline.* You're not solving a murder. You're clocking enough human signal to sound real.

Work priority accounts for 30 days with 12+ touches. Enough to matter. Not enough to become folklore.

Then move promising threads into real-time, fast. The second there's life, move it toward phone, text, WhatsApp, voice note, or a live hold. Email is where people cosplay thoughtfulness for days. Real-time channels expose the truth faster. That's where you find out whether there's actual energy or just clean grammar.

That's why call blocks matter. If you're an AE, hit 8 a.m. and 4 p.m. If you're an SDR, think 9 a.m., 1 p.m., and 4 p.m. Or just run two focused two-hour blocks, one morning, one afternoon. Doesn't matter what religion you pick. Rhythm matters more than doctrine. You need enough live contact that your nervous system stops treating every decent reply like it's a solar eclipse.

Then aim for resistance, not comfort. Try to get 3 to 4 "no" responses over time in your cold call and DM interactions. No resistance usually means no real conversation. Real conversations have texture. Pushback. Slight discomfort. If everybody's being perfectly polite, there's a decent chance nobody's actually in it.

That's a feature, not a bug.

Also, maintain professional etiquette like an adult. If someone says don't contact me, remove them immediately. There's a difference between calibrated persistence and becoming the office cautionary tale.

Finally, tune the machine constantly. A/B test personalization angle, send time, channel order, voicemail style, opener, CTA, and connection path. Not because optimization is your higher calling, but because markets shift, buyers shift, and stale confidence is how average reps turn into content creators explaining why their quarter was "a learning experience."

That's the loop.

Run it every business day, and you'll give yourself something most reps never build: Enough live motion to develop feel.

And feel is what lets you catch timing before it turns into hindsight.

TAKEAWAY: IF YOU FEEL IT, MOVE

There's one story in here that keeps repeating in different outfits.

A conversation was clearly moving. The energy was rising. The signals were aligning. A point arrived where the next step wasn't something to invent, just something to recognize. And instead of recognizing it, somebody stepped back into their head. They optimized. They refined.

They delayed just long enough for reality to cool. Then, once it did, they spent the rest of the interaction trying to recreate the original heat with increasingly reasonable language.

Momentum isn't stable. It's alive.

It either continues through you or leaves without you. There's no neutral.

When the room shifts, your brain offers you two paths.

One says: respond to what's alive.

The other says: reduce your own risk.

Most people pick the second and call it discipline.

That's why they say things like:

- "I didn't want to push too hard."
- "I wanted to be thoughtful."
- "I didn't want to make it weird."
- "I figured I'd send something over and let them think."

Sure.

And by the time they think, the energy that would've carried the next move is gone. Optionality enters the room. Real life reasserts itself. Desire hires caution as its lawyer. What should've been a continuation now has to be sold back into a colder reality.

So the practical rule is simple: when the room shifts from browsing to transition, move with it before your fear turns the moment into admin.

First, learn to spot the turn. The room's probably opening when the questions get more specific, the tone gets tighter, they stop asking what it does and start asking how it works for them, and they bring up stakeholders, rollout, timing, ownership, or internal friction. That's not random engagement. That's a shift. If you miss that shift and keep explaining, you're not being thoughtful.

You're arriving late.

Second, stop killing live moments with extra explanation. When the room turns, don't add a recap, stack more proof, keep teaching, or soften your language until it sounds like customer success in a eucalyptus-scented coworking space.

That's how you turn chemistry into onboarding.

Instead, say the next thing:

- "Feels like we've moved past theory here."
- "This sounds worth pressure-testing live."
- "If this is real, let's stop talking around it."
- "Easier to walk through than explain."
- "Tomorrow at two or Thursday morning?"
- "Who else should be in that room if this is live?"

That's escalation done correctly.

It feels like continuity.

Third, know when you're too early. You're probably escalating too soon when they're still asking broad educational questions. They haven't owned the problem. Maybe the next step would feel like a jump instead of a continuation. Maybe your body knows you're reacting more to your own adrenaline than to the room.

That's when you don't force it.

You ask one more clean question:

- "Where's that showing up most?"
- "What happens if nothing changes?"
- "Who actually feels that internally?"
- "Is that annoying, or expensive?"

That's how you let the interaction earn the next move.

Fourth, use the loop without worshipping it. The operating loop is there to build exposure, not to make you sound templated. Use it to create enough live reps, signal density, and real contact that timing becomes recognizable. Build surface area daily. Act on signals daily. Get into real-time channels early. Vary your touch pattern so you don't become wallpaper.

The loop gets you into enough motion to recognize the shift.

You still have to *move* when it appears.

CHAPTER 11:
C-LEVEL SEDUCTION: POWER RECOGNIZES POWER INSTANTLY

"We are each of us angels with only one wing, and we can only fly by embracing one another."

– Luciano De Crescenzo

You're not supposed to get this meeting.

Not in this timeline. Not in *this economy*. Not in a world where assistants gatekeep like they're guarding the last Infinity Stone.

This is C-level.

This is velvet-rope energy.

This is "if you have to ask, you're not on the list" energy.

This is the part of the org where people act like calendars are military installations and your quick intro note dies somewhere between legal, golf, and an unread folder called "later, maybe never."

And yet you dial anyway.

Because somewhere between logic and delusion, you've realized something most people never do: access isn't granted, it's taken cleanly.

Power doesn't give you a warm runway. It doesn't invite you to build relevance slowly like you're laying out brunch. It decides, almost instantly, whether you feel like signal or effort. Whether you sound like a person who sees something real, or just another overprepared adult child with a polished deck and a sentence that starts with "I wanted to reach out because..."

That's why most people lose before the conversation even starts.

Not because they're wrong. Because they feel like work. And executives hate work that arrives disguised as politeness.

The phone rings. He picks up.

"Yeah."

No warmth. No curiosity. No hello. Just raw, uncut executive bandwidth. He's mid-flight, mid-deal, mid-life. You're not scheduled. You're not expected. You are, in his world, a glitch with a country code.

Most people hear that tone and instantly fold like a cheap lawn chair at a backyard barbecue. They panic-introduce themselves like they're reading a LinkedIn bio under duress. They start explaining, over-contexting, over-apologizing, like they just walked into the wrong classroom and decided the best move was a presentation about why.

That's how you lose in under three seconds.

So you don't do that.

You drop straight into the line.

"Are you still pushing that transformation initiative, or did it stall?"

Pause.

Not a polite pause. Not a thoughtful pause. The kind of pause that means the room just changed shape, and he knows it.

"Who is this?"

Flat. Surgical. Security-checkpoint energy.

And right here is where ninety-nine percent of people turn into anxious teenagers begging for approval. They scramble. They explain. They start speaking in that awful adult-schoolboy tone people use when talking to power, half respectful, half submissive, fully dead on arrival.

You don't.

"Someone who's seen how those usually go sideways. Figured it was worth asking before it locks in."

At that level, nobody cares how polished you sound. Everyone sounds polished. That's the problem. Executives aren't filtering for polish. They're filtering for compression. They want the shortest possible route to consequence, risk, leverage, misalignment, or hidden cost.

They don't want more information; they want fast gratification.

Then comes the classic exit line, delivered like muscle memory:

"Look, I'm about to step into something."

Click.

Disconnected. Ghosted. Cut off by the man himself. Left on read by reality.

And this is where most people emotionally fall apart. They log it. They cope. They tell themselves it was close, which is the professional version of saying, "No, but the vibe was good." They convert the loss into a little bedtime story about how, at least, they got him live.

No.

You don't spiral.

You don't send a follow-up paragraph that reads like a man trying to explain why he should still be in the club after the bouncer already looked at his shoes.

You call again.

Not aggressively. Not emotionally like you're trying to convince a dealer it's "safe" to sell to you again after your last overdose. Like nothing happened. Like the first call was a trailer and this is the actual movie.

Ring.

"Yeah."

Slight shift. Tiny, but there. Like someone who ignored you once and suddenly realizes you might not be ignorable.

"Quick one. If that initiative's still active, you're about to see the pipeline inflate and then quietly degrade underneath it."

Now you've done it.

You introduced tension.

"What do you mean?"

There it is.

You didn't open the door. You changed the room temperature.

"It'll look good up top. Board buys in. Hiring spikes. Activity goes up. But underneath, it falls apart. Different teams are solving different versions of the same problem. You get discord instead of alignment."

Pause.

"Yeah."

That "yeah" is everything. It's recognition. It's him mentally checking a box he didn't realize needed checking.

"Keep going."

And just like that, you're in.

Not because you impressed him. Not because you dazzled him with charisma or made him laugh or gave him your best TEDx voice.

Because you named something real.

And you named it *before* he had to do the work of explaining it to himself.

This is the real difference between selling upward and selling everywhere else. Mid-level buyers will sometimes indulge effort. They'll read the paragraph. They'll sit through the explanation. They'll let you be thorough. Senior leaders won't.

Not because they're cruel. Because they're compressed, they're the "hottest matches" on Tinder, trying to find someone worth talking to amongst a sea of requests for "nudes" and the same six "funny" opening lines on repeat.

Thoughtful messages feel like something that needs to be reviewed, which means they get mentally parked next to unread newsletters, abandoned gym memberships, and every app someone meant to delete three iPhones ago.

Senior leaders don't ignore you because you're wrong.

They ignore you because you feel like effort.

And effort at that level is everywhere. It's flooding the inbox. It's cc'd on everything. It's "wanted to reach out…" and "thought this might be relevant…" and "given your recent strategic priorities…" and "hope this finds you well," which is the corporate equivalent of showing up to a gunfight with a fruit platter and a compliance-approved smile.

Signal cuts through because it doesn't ask for time.

It interrupts it.

That's what Miranda Priestly does in a room. That's what a good *Succession* line does. That's what a properly sharp executive opener does. It lands before it explains. It creates a moment before it creates understanding. It forces the other person to lean in just to stabilize the frame.

"You're probably focused on the wrong lever."

"This is either noise or leverage."

"That initiative usually looks healthy right before it flat lines."

"You're solving the visible problem, not the expensive one."

Those lines don't chase. They sit there like a line in a *Gone Girl* monologue, unsettling in exactly the right way, precise enough to make the other person feel something before they've had time to formally disagree.

And that's the trick.

C-level doesn't reward effort.

It rewards compression.

The more words you need to establish your relevance, the less relevance you had.

The moment you rush to clarify, you collapse the thing that made it powerful.

Restraint is the actual flex.

Anyone can say more. Very few people can create a live moment and then not smother it because silence makes them itchy.

But if you learn anything from Fez in *Euphoria*, it should be this: Silence isn't a leak you need to patch.

Silence is where the other person starts doing the work.

"This is where it breaks."

And then you let it sit.

Not because you're playing games. Because if the point is real, they will step into it.

If it isn't, they won't.

Need is loud.

Need is the extra sentence. The nervous laugh. The fast reply. The "totally understand, just wanted to quickly…" The verbal kneeling. The impulse to prove you belong in the room after the room already told you it would decide for itself.

Need repels.

Certainty is quieter than that.

Certainty is the person who says less and means more. The one who can let a moment sit without rushing to rescue it. The one who doesn't need this interaction to validate their existence because they already behave like someone who wins most of them.

"This isn't something we need to keep talking about if it's not a priority."

That line lands differently when it's true. No chasing. No trying to emotionally invoice the other person for your effort like they owe you a reply because you were brave enough to use Outlook.

And that's the paradox.

The moment you're willing to lose is the moment you become the only one who can win.

That sounds like something people would over-post with a black-and-white photo and the word grit in the caption, but unfortunately, it's true. The second you stop needing the outcome to validate your presence, your signal changes. You stop talking to power like you need permission. You stop earning relevance in real time, which is good, because the moment you start earning it, you've already lowered the frame.

Power doesn't respond to effort.

Power responds to power.

And power, in this context, is certainty without permission.

TAKEAWAY: CONNECTING WITH THE "ABSOLUTE TENS"

If you're reaching out to senior leaders, the standard is brutally simple: Don't sound like effort.

That means no long setup. No apology. No biography. No "hope you're doing well." No warm little runway where you try to prove you were raised right and understand punctuation. Executives don't need your respectful tone. They need a reason not to mentally archive you with the other thoughtful little messages they'll never open again.

Lead with signal.

Bad:

"Hi John, hope you're well. I wanted to reach out because we help organizations undergoing transformation..."

Better:

"Transformation usually looks healthy right before it shatters."

Bad:

"I noticed your recent initiative and thought this might be relevant..."

Better:

"You're probably focused on the wrong lever."

Bad:

"We work with companies like yours to drive alignment across teams…"

Better:

"Your teams are probably solving different versions of the same problem right now."

When they respond coldly, and they often will, don't panic. If they say, "Who is this?" don't launch into your resume. If they say "Yeah," don't start tap-dancing. If they say they're busy or they cut the call short, don't turn it into a full tarot reading over call recordings and a $9 espresso. Stay brief. Stay flat. Stay inside the frame.

- "Someone who's seen how these usually go sideways."
- "Quick one."
- "If it's not live, I'll leave it."

If it needs to be processed, it's probably dead. If it feels like a point of view compressed into one unsettlingly clear line, you're closer.

Also, don't fill the silence just because silence makes you uncomfortable. Silence is where the executive decides whether what you said is real. If you jump in too fast, all you're doing is proving you don't trust your own line enough to let it land.

And when you follow up, don't turn into a loyal little background character in their inbox. No "just checking in." No "wanted to float this back up." No emotional residue. Every touch should feel like a fresh signal, not persistence theater.

Good executive follow-up sounds like:

- "Still looks like the same risk."
- "This either matters now or it doesn't."
- "The visible issue probably still isn't the expensive one."
- "Worth revisiting before it locks in."

Short. Sparse. Point-of-view driven. No verbal kneeling.

The would-be love interest you're pursuing doesn't need more messages telling them how "hot" they are. Executives don't need more respect.

They need *more signal.*

They don't need the polished version of your effort.

They need the compressed version of your nerve.

So go in clean. Name something real. Don't explain it to death. Don't react to coldness. Don't earn relevance in real time.

Because the second you stop talking to power like you need permission, power starts hearing you differently.

CONCLUSION:

THE ONE WHO WAS NEVER TRYING TO WIN

"I am not what happened to me, I am what I choose to become."

– Carl Jung

By now, you probably know this book was never really about prospecting.

Not *only* prospecting, anyway.

It wasn't really about cold calls, emails, DMs, LinkedIn, objection handling, follow-ups, or any of the other respectable little labels people use when they want human behavior to sound less human and more like a software category. Those were just the outfits. The machinery underneath was always the same: attention, tension, timing, presence, restraint, and the tiny silent decision between moving with what's alive or trying to force what isn't.

That's the whole book. Nothing says modern romance like a profound spiritual connection plus a strong urge not to double-text.

And if I'm honest, the clearest version of it didn't happen in a boardroom, or on a sales floor, or inside some beautifully optimized sequence with a 41 percent open rate and a subject line a RevOps guy wanted to bronze and hang in the lobby.

It happened when I met my wife.

Which, yes, sounds dangerously sincere after a whole book of calling bad outreach spiritually dead and comparing pipeline to situationships.

Stay with me. The irony is part of the fun.

The first time I saw her, she was doing a podcast with one of my mentors, my spiritual mentor. And the second I saw her, I felt the inclination to reach out.

Not "I considered the strategic upside."

I felt it.

So I reached out, because I always fearlessly reach out.

Most people spend half their lives manufacturing reasons to move when the real reason was already there. They felt the pull. They noticed the shift. They saw the thing. But instead of trusting that, they start workshopping reality like it's a QBR deck that still needs three revisions, a logo cleanup, and one deeply unnecessary sentence about "synergy."

That's how they miss the first live moment.

I reached out. And I didn't get much back.

She clearly wasn't interested in me at the time. It is what it is. *This was 2020.*

This is where most people would reveal whether they've learned anything at all. A lot of people can reach out once. Far fewer can hear no without turning it into a Greek tragedy, a revenge gym arc, or six paragraphs in Notes App titled "clarity."

Most reps treat "no" like one of two things. Either it's a death sentence, and they collapse. Or it's secretly negotiable, so they chase. They become the guy still trying to make "just wanted to bump this" feel sexy six emails later.

I didn't do that.

I moved on with my life.

No hard feelings. No trying to squeeze a yes out of a closed door because my ego wanted one more audition.

That is one of the hardest lessons in this whole book.

No doesn't always mean never.

A lot of the time, it means *not now.*

Then, in March 2021, I saw her post something on Facebook, and I sent her a meme.

Naturally.

I didn't send, "Hey, just checking in." I didn't write, "I wanted to circle back on our previous conversation." I didn't show up in her digital life, sounding like a customer success rep trying to resurrect Q3.

I sent a meme.

Presence. Play. Timing. Re-entry without residue.

When the door reopened, I didn't come back dragging continuity debt behind me like an overstuffed carry-on full of my previous disappointment. I entered clean. Light. Alive. Human.

And from that day, the conversation never stopped.

That matters too, because people love romanticizing the wrong things. They imagine some giant breakthrough moment, some cinematic pivot, some one-line closer where everything changes at once, and *Labrinth* starts playing in the background like we're all suddenly in *Euphoria* with better skin and worse decision-making.

Usually it's not like that.

Usually, it's simpler. Cleaner. Stranger. The conversation just kept moving because both people were actually in it. There was mutual pull. Real energy. Life. It didn't need to be dragged forward like a weak deal in a forecast call where everyone's pretending "they asked for the deck" means something.

It kept moving because it was alive.

And the way it felt in my body was intense. A constant state of happiness, aliveness, certainty, and yes, something ecstatic and overwhelming in it too. That's the honest truth. But here's the part that matters most:

I still had to regulate myself.

People miss that because they think the presence of strong feelings is what ruins the interaction. It isn't. Strong feelings are not the problem. The problem is dysregulation. The problem is when the feeling takes the wheel and starts acting for you. That's when people spray. Over-email. Over-call. Over-text. Over-signal. Over-clarify. Over-promise. They feel the energy and then immediately convert it into pressure.

That's how they kill the thing they care about.

I had to make sure I was there for her in a way where I could hold space and give, not take.

That's not just a love lesson.

That's the whole damn book.

A grounded seller feels the room and doesn't lunge. A grounded man feels desire and doesn't rush to secure it. A grounded operator feels certainty and still has the discipline not to turn it into theater.

The first time we ever met on Zoom was because we were talking about marketing, and I wanted to help Hannah in her business. That was the frame.

On paper.

In reality, when we got on the call, we barely talked about marketing. We just kept looking at each other and breathing for hours. Eight hours.

That will sound insane to some people.

Fine.

Let it.

Because that moment makes the argument of this whole book more clearly than any chapter could. The agenda fell away, and what was left was presence.

That Zoom call worked because nobody was wrenching it toward a tidy outcome. The close happened by itself.

That's one of the strangest truths in the world, whether we're talking love or pipeline: when something is actually real, the next move rarely feels like force. It feels like a continuation. Like the next beat in a song that was already playing.

On the second Zoom call, I told her the truth.

"I don't want to be a third wheel."

Since she was married, that had to dissolve for us to be together.

Now that's not a soft line. It's also not manipulative.

It's clarity.

And clarity is one of the most misunderstood forces in both sales and dating. People think directness is pressure. Usually, the opposite is true. Ambiguity is what creates anxiety. Endless vagueness is what makes people feel unsafe. Dripping, blurry, "let's just see" energy is what turns interactions into emotional admin because the truth is clearly in the room, but nobody's saying it out loud.

I wasn't pleading. I wasn't gaming. I wasn't waiting three months hoping she'd decode my vibe and make the move for me. I wasn't pretending patience while secretly rotting inside uncertainty and calling it depth.

I said the true thing.

Then I let reality answer.

That's qualification, escalation, and boundary setting all at once.

That's the moment where most reps lose their nerve and replace truth with "totally fine either way, just wanted to see if maybe perhaps..." because they're terrified the direct ask will scare the prospect away.

Sometimes it will.

Good.

Things that aren't real should leave sooner.

The right people, the right deals, the right moments often move faster after clarity, not slower. Because directness doesn't create tension, it reveals it.

And once something real is revealed, decisions compress.

She moved out the same day.

My yearning and my boundary were honored.

Then we met in Mexico for the first time in person in June.

And I could see her under the light like an angel. The image stayed with me. Still does.

Within minutes, I put a ring on her.

Yes. Ooh, scary marriage. Very dramatic. Very, "are we allowed to say that in a book about prospecting?" Apparently, we are.

Because I knew she was *the one* from the day we started talking.

That line is going to make some people deeply uncomfortable.

Because it tears straight through the timid little bureaucracy people build around certainty. They train themselves to ask permission from the room before they'll admit what they know. They need consensus. Confirmation. A few more data points. A panel review. Three trusted advisors and perhaps a color-coded Notion board titled *discernment.*

But certainty moves faster than permission.

That doesn't mean recklessness. It means that when something is actually real, actually aligned, actually clear, the next move doesn't come from begging reality to validate it.

It comes from naming it.

That's why so much of what passes for selling is exhausting. It's one person trying to manufacture motion where none exists. It's maintenance. Performance. Grasping. The whole nervous system lunging toward reassurance and then calling it strategy because strategy sounds smarter and less like abandonment issues in a CRM.

Real movement feels different.

Cleaner.

Faster.

Less needy.

No *bending the knee.* No begging. No trying to negotiate your way into being chosen.

Then we moved back to Santa Barbara, and seven months from June, we got married.

Small wedding. Fourteen guests. At the Bluff.

And none of that was really the point.

The point was us.

That's another thing people miss in selling. They get distracted by the audience, optics, process, performance, and the appearance of momentum. They start serving the theater instead of the thing itself.

The best deals don't feel like theater. The best relationships don't either.

They feel like the signal got clean enough that all the extra machinery could finally fall away.

And there's another lesson hidden in it that matters just as much: Fearless reach-out means nothing without fearless release.

That's the dance.

Presence, space, presence, space.

The rep who only reaches out becomes a stalker with a sequencer. The rep who only lets go becomes passive and calls it detachment. A real operator can do both.

Move when something calls you.

Leave when it's not alive.

Return cleanly when the door opens.

Name what's true when the room can carry it.

Don't smother the moment because your ego needs closure faster than reality wants to give it.

That's pipeline. That's love. That's power.

If I had to compress the whole book into one sentence, it would probably be this:

The one who wins is never really the one trying hardest to win.

It's the one who can see clearly, move cleanly, and not need the outcome to explain who they are.

You can't fake the absence of need for very long. You can fake confidence. You can fake cleverness. You can fake certainty for about three messages and half a call. But you can't fake what happens when somebody genuinely no longer needs the moment to go a certain way to remain whole.

That's when everything changes.

You stop sounding like effort. You stop forcing heat into cold rooms. You stop trying to rescue things that never had enough tension to move.

And then, finally, the work gets simpler.

You stop trying to win. You start trying to see.

That's when people trust you, when power hears you, and synchronicities appear as if by magic.

That's when the next move starts feeling obvious instead of scary.

And that's when the close, whether it's a meeting, a deal, a life partner, or one of those terrifyingly serious adult decisions everybody pretends to be cool about, stops feeling like a conquest.

It's inevitable.

Stop chasing, and watch what starts choosing you.

Shoutout to Rebekah Carter for turning up the heat on this book with Euphoria-level hypnotic savagery and somehow making us feel things we weren't planning on feeling, and to Muzammil Yaqoob for the eye-catching cover design.

Thank you for spending your time with this book.

If you enjoyed what you read, the greatest compliment you can give is sharing your thoughts with other readers. Even a few sentences about your experience can help someone decide whether this book is right for them.

Your support means more than you know.

Thank you for being part of this journey.

www.ingramcontent.com/pod-product-compliance
Lightning Source LLC
LaVergne TN
LVHW022044200926
848481LV00003B/784